Tibetan Cooking

Recipes for Daily Living, Celebration, and Ceremony

Tibetan Cooking

Recipes for Daily Living, Celebration, and Ceremony

Elizabeth Esther Kelly

Snow Lion Publications
Ithaca, New York
Boulder, Colorado

Snow Lion Publications
P.O. Box 6483
Ithaca, NY 14851 USA
(607) 273-8519
www.snowlionpub.com

Printed in Canada on acid-free recycled paper.

ISBN-10: 1-55939-262-2
ISBN-13: 978-1-55939-262-4

Library of Congress Cataloging-in-Publication Data

Kelly, Elizabeth Esther, 1950-
 Tibetan cooking : recipes for daily living, celebration, and ceremony /
Elizabeth Esther Kelly.
    p. cm.
 ISBN-13: 978-1-55939-262-4 (alk. paper)
 ISBN-10: 1-55939-262-2 (alk. paper)
 1. Cookery, Tibetan. I. Title.
TX724.5.T55K45 2007
641.5951'5–dc22
                            2007018541

Spot illustrations by Palden Oshoe; chapter heading drawings by
the author. Designed by Wendy Kenigsberg.

Dedication

THIS BOOK IS DEDICATED TO UNWAVERING BELIEF IN ENDING WORLD HUNGER AND CULTIVATING WORLD PEACE.

Acknowledgments

With gratitude for the Grace of the Guru, thanks to all who have been patient with me and who have taught me patience. Love and appreciation to James and Alice Kelly, Caesar and Lucy Nosenzo, my children Esme and James, Ama Dronlha and all my Tibetan family. Thanks to Harper Blanchett for his wonderful black-and-white photographs.

TABLE of CONTENTS

Tibetan Cooking vii

Introduction

While this is a cookbook about Tibetan food, the real subject is love. The inspiration has come from love and, as it is often said, "God is love." My mother would say, "The way to a man's heart is through his stomach," and I saw her faithfully prepare meal after meal with love for her family every single day of the week, year after year, satisfied with her work.

My interest in Tibetan food and its intrinsic connection to the divine was sparked one late summer afternoon in 1978. Venerable Lama Norlha, a deeply inspiring teacher, was visiting my humble home in the mountains. He had just arrived from India, invited by a Buddhist student and mutual friend. Before having lunch together, Lama looked around the kitchen for a cup of some kind. Without the benefit of a mutual language, we found a stemmed dessert glass. This we set on a saucer and in the glass poured some fresh black tea to overflowing. Lama then placed it on the window sill above the counter and said "Mahakala," the name of the dharma protector of our lineage.

I was deeply moved by Lama Norhla's devotion, adhering to his formal practice although far removed from any familiar place. I was very grateful to know that a bit of boiled water with a pinch of tea was enough, an acceptable offering due the reverent manner in which it was given, and also to learn from this example that one can integrate one's practice into daily life with grace and simplicity. This offering, linking the divine and the mundane, sanctified not only that meal but also the life-supporting sustenance provided by all our daily meals.

Many years later I married my husband Gala, a carpet master from Eastern Tibet. Traditionally, Tibetan men are not cooks, but during his childhood in a refugee settlement in the northern wilderness of Nepal, he had learned many skills, among them cooking. He promptly saw the advantage of teaching me his favorite dishes and techniques.

Learning was easy, because I had grown up cooking with my grandmother, and have always loved to cook. Every Sunday after church we would come home to a house that smelled of herbs, roasted meat, and potatoes. It was a special time, when the whole family had a late lunch together and enjoyed a day of rest. My father was home from work and we wore our best clothes. The associations of singing, incense and flowers in church, and the comfort of my grandmother's cooking have stayed with me as a grounded path and another link between the sacred and the ordinary.

When preparing food for large numbers of people, a group effort is required. Tibetan families are generally large, and preparing food together is part of the natural flow of life. It becomes fun: the process of preparing a meal is social and also gets done faster this way. Most traditional foods, being made from scratch, are not instant or easy but the more you do anything, the easier it becomes. An entire day may be spent congenially cooking and eating, mixed with laughter and song.

Gala has told me many stories over the years of the times when food was not readily available. His mother had to trade her jewelry and traditional hair ornaments for food. The story of his family's three-year journey on foot, running for their lives from the Communist Chinese army, is a poignant one. During his family's transition from impoverished circumstances in exile to the relative security of the modern world, food has been central to survival, both physically and spiritually. As he says, "People practice dharma when they have food enough."

Gala's family comes from the eastern part of the Tibetan plateau where tribal peoples have lived for generations, managing herds of goats, sheep, yaks, and horses. Everything that was needed—food, clothing, and shelter—derived from the animals. The diet consisted of dairy products: milk, butter, various forms of dried cheese, and yogurt, as well as dried meat and the roasted barley flour called tsampa. Every moment of the day was spent in some aspect of survival and main-taining the food supply, beginning each morning with milking the animals. Families moved alongside their animals to different grazing areas on a cyclical basis. During yak caravans stretching over several months, the staples not grown in the region were obtained through barter. Wool and butter were traded for barley, salt, and tea.

Everything essential to the life of these nomads came from the land that supported the grazing herds. Butter was stored inside a leather bag, sewn from a goat's skin. This could hold about one hundred pounds and would serve as a sustaining gift to a local monastery. The people living close to the earth provided all the food for the lamas and monks, who were then free to read the texts and practice the Buddha Dharma, the treasure of Tibetan culture. In turn, the spiritual life of the nomads was nourished by the spiritual practice of the lamas and monks. The people relied on the lamas in all life-changing decisions and in the critical times of sickness, birth, and death.

This past spring, a powerful transition occurred in our own home and Tibetan food was central to the process of healing. Gala suddenly became ill and his life was threatened. The ancient ways of healing with herbal medicine, food, and prayer gave him back his life. We found a Tibetan doctor who was also a lama. Fortunately he was able to come to our home immediately, carrying many medicinal herbs with him in a huge bag. He performed the diagnosis, made the prescription, and conducted the appropriate puja. This process took all day. The lama then prescribed a course of treatment to follow.

Many visitors came to our home to wish Gala well, all appearing with bags of food: fresh vegetables hard to find in our area and abundant staples and beverages to serve other visitors. Many foods were offered through multiple pujas: whole grains, butter, honey, meat, sugar, and spirits. The abundance of good will represented in the offering of food was intended to remove obstacles and clear the way for recovery. Ironically, while all this food was coming into our home, my husband had to fast on a diet of thin rice soup and take herbal medicine around the clock. At times the absence of food is what creates balance. Meanwhile, family and friends gathered to feast and cook, providing inspiration to live and recover.

This situation exemplified the integrated relationship between sustenance and survival. While it is no mystery that people have to eat to live, it has always impressed me that water, food, and fasting are prominent in many Tibetan Buddhist ritual ceremonies. At times those present eat the consecrated food and at other times the consecrated food is burnt as an offering. Realizing that food is not just a metaphor for spiritual nourishment but is itself spiritual, we can prepare and eat food with the appropriate intention. In so doing, the body, speech, and mind are nourished.

Meal Planning

Traditional Eastern Tibetan meals consisted of all natural, organic foods. The methods of preserving meats and dairy products were also completely natural. Every part of the animal was utilized. The diet was perfect for the vigorous life of a nomadic people living on the Tibetan plateau. The staple diet was roasted barley flour, called tsampa, butter tea, yogurt, and dried meat. Once in exile, their way of living and eating changed dramatically.

In times past, the sign of a special Tibetan meal was a large number of dishes. Guests would be served small portions of a variety of dishes, one or two at a time, served in small bowls and covered cups. This custom is still observed at Losar, the Tibetan New Year. On a daily basis Tibetan food is fairly simple and very often the meal consists of one dish. This is particularly true of the soups, such as tukpa, which are very hearty. Momos, which are the most renowned Tibetan dish, are also a one-dish meal. Momos are traditionally served with condiments alone, but balancing the meal with steamed greens or a green salad will be appreciated by Tibetans and Westerners alike, especially if the momos are filled with meat.

It is not impolite to inquire about dietary preferences or restrictions when inviting Tibetan guests for a meal. Ask the lama's attendant for this information if you are planning to invite your teacher. You will then know how many vegetarians will attend and can balance the meal accordingly. Some Tibetan monks and lamas are vegetarians, but most do eat meat. Fish is the animal eaten least among Tibetans. Beef, lamb, and pork, being large animals, are preferred because offering the life of only one of these animals feeds many humans. In traditional monastic settings the main meal is still taken at noon, so lunch invitations are often preferable.

A large pot of rice will take care of holding any meal together. Tibetans enjoy a large plate of rice, and a little of everything else that is served. If meat is the main dish, cook more than you think is necessary. Meat can always be served cold with condiments later on, instead of dessert. No doubt there are a few Tibetans of the younger generation who love sweets, but in general, freshly cut oranges and yogurt after the meal will be most welcome. Tibetans are often interested in any family recipes you may have to offer, or ethnic specialties that they have never tried.

The serving suggestions included with many recipes in this book will help with meal planning. Be creative! If the food is prepared with love, it will be perfect.

Mealtime Prayer

I pay homage to the Buddha, Precious Teacher

I pay homage to the Dharma, Precious Sangha

I pay homage to the Sangha, Precious Community

To the Three Jewels, I offer my merit

DUN PA LA ME SANG JE RINPOCHE

CHO PA LA ME DAM CHO RINPOCHE

DREN PA LA ME GEN DUN RINPOCHE

KYAP NE KUN SHO SUM LA CHO PA BUL

Bread and Rice

STEAMED ROLLS

Timo

SERVES 6 TO 8

Timo are often served in place of rice, and are especially good with dishes that have gravy, such as curries. They may be eaten hot or cold. Left-over timo may be pan-fried for breakfast. Break the timo into smaller pieces and toss in light oil or butter till they become crunchy. Children, and those fond of sweets, may enjoy timo shredded into a bowl with melted butter and honey.

INGREDIENTS:

8 cups unbleached white flour
4 teaspoons baking powder
½ teaspoon baking soda
2 cups cold water

Sift the dry ingredients together in a bowl.

Gradually incorporate the water into the flour mixture by slowly pouring it into the center while mixing in a circular motion from the center outward. When the dough has formed, knead about five minutes until it is soft and pliable. It should not be sticky.

Let the dough rest 20 to 30 minutes, covered with a bowl or plastic.

Roll the dough out flat about ¼ inch thick, using the minimum amount of flour necessary.

Oil the surface of the dough lightly and then cut the entire shape into strips 2 to 3 inches wide and about 8 inches long. Fold and twist each piece into a pleasing shape and place on a lightly oiled steamer tray, arranging the timo so they are not touching.

Heat the water in the bottom of the steamer. When the water is rapidly boiling, place the steamer trays on top, cover, and steam undisturbed for 15 minutes.

Keep any left-over timo in a plastic bag or air tight container or they will become hard and dry very quickly. Usually they disappear very quickly!

SWEET BREAD
Ngamo Palep
SERVES 4 TO 6

This bread is usually made for breakfast. The early riser or designated breakfast cook can have this on the table in thirty minutes.

INGREDIENTS:

3 cups unbleached white flour
2 teaspoons baking powder
1 pinch baking soda
1 cup very warm water
¼ to ⅓ cup sugar

Sift the flour, baking powder, and baking soda together. Measure the sugar into a 1-cup measuring cup and then fill the cup with warm water, stirring to dissolve the sugar.

Mix the sugar water into the flour, working from the center outward. The dough will be soft and sticky.

Knead the dough for a few minutes. Roll it out into a circle that fits the bottom of a 12-inch iron pan, about 1 to 1½ inches thick.

Cover the ngamo palep while you heat the iron pan with ¼ inch of cooking oil. Before placing the dough in the pan, pierce it with a sharp knife, making two cuts about 4 inches long. This will insure even cooking.

Cook over medium to low heat, being careful not to burn it. Rotate the bread in the pan every 30 seconds.

When a crust begins to form on the bottom after about 5 minutes, turn the bread over using two large spatulas. Repeat this process to promote even cooking. It will rise slightly.

Ngamo palep is considered done when tapping it with the knuckles produces a certain hollow sound. After a few tries you will recognize it.

Turn the ngamo palep out onto a cutting board and cut it into small rectangular pieces, one by two inches. It is very filling, and delicious with Tibetan tea.

FRIED MEAT-FILLED BREADS
Sha Palep

SERVES 4 TO 6

Sha palep is essentially a cooked sandwich, formed by two rounds of bread filled with meat. Sha palep are very filling, and can be served as a main dish. Usually one prepares enough to have some left, as they are a delicious snack served cold with the hot chili sauce called martza (see p. 65). The durable construction makes sha palep an easy-to-pack food, great to take on picnics or for box lunches.

INGREDIENTS:

Dough:
4 cups unbleached white flour
½ cup whole wheat flour
I cup cold water

Filling:
I pound fresh ground beef
½ cube beef bouillon
½ bunch fresh cilantro – ½ cup chopped
½ bunch fresh scallions – ½ cup chopped
salt or soy sauce to taste

Prepare the dough by incorporating the cold water into the combined flours, mixing well and kneading by hand. Cover the dough and let rest for 15 to 20 minutes while you prepare the filling.

Place the meat in a small mixing bowl. Add the bouillon cube dissolved in ½ cup hot water. Finely chop the cilantro and scallions and add them to the meat. Knead this mixture with your hands until it is well blended.

When the filling is ready, roll out the dough to about 1/8-inch thickness and cut into 4-inch circles, using a glass or cookie cutter.

Spread filling evenly about ½ inch thick on the surface of one circle, leaving about a ½ inch of space around the edge. Cover with a second plain circle and seal by twisting the edges together, as one might crimp the edge of a pie shell.

Place the completed sha palep on a plate, being careful not to let them touch each other, or they will stick together.

To save time, you may begin to heat about ¼ inch of oil in a cast iron frying pan over medium heat, and start frying the sha palep once you have a few made. (I like to cover the pan for a few minutes also, to steam the meat inside.) It takes about 10 minutes to cook through.

Place the cooked sha palep on a plate covered with a paper towel to absorb the extra oil. Cover to keep them warm. Sha palep are good served with steamed greens or salad and hot sauce.

SWEET FILLED STEAMED ROLLS
Desi Palep

SERVES 4 TO 6

This form of bread is essentially a version of timo, or Steamed Rolls, found on page 2. It makes a very filling breakfast along with Tibetan tea, a salty complement, or with yogurt. It takes more than one hour to prepare.

INGREDIENTS:

Dough:
8 cups unbleached white flour
4 teaspoons baking powder
½ teaspoon baking soda
2 cups cold water

Filling #1:
2 cups cooked Tibetan wild yams (dhoma; see p. 101)
¼ cup unsalted butter

Filling #2:
1 16 oz. can cooked red beans
½ cup maple syrup
⅛ cup unsalted butter

Sift the dry ingredients together in a bowl.

Gradually incorporate the water into the flour mixture by slowly pouring it into the center while mixing in a circular motion from the center outward. When the dough has formed, knead about five minutes until it is soft and pliable. It should not be sticky.

Let the dough rest 20 to 30 minutes, covered with a bowl or plastic. While the dough is resting, prepare the filling.

FILLING #1:

Melt the butter and mash it together with the cooked dhoma until a smooth paste is formed. The natural sweetness and flavor of the dhoma makes a very special and distinctive filling, similar to chestnut.

FILLING #2:

Blend the beans, syrup, and butter in a blender and you will have a fine, rich filling that resembles dhoma. Very easy.

Roll out the dough about ½ inch thick. Cut the dough into 4-inch circles.

In the center of each circle place 1 teaspoon of filling. Twist and pinch the circle closed. Place in an oiled steamer.

Steam for 20 minutes. Serve immediately.

SCALLION PANCAKE
Tsey Paklep

SERVES 4 TO 6

These pancakes can be a meal in themselves for light eaters. They need only a simple soup or salad to make a filling lunch or dinner. It takes an hour to prepare these, and some facility with the rolling pin. Well worth the effort. The extra ones can be stored and reheated.

INGREDIENTS:

> 8 cups unbleached white flour
> 4 cups cold water
> 1 bunch scallions
> 1 small onion
> salt
> Five Spice powder (optional)
> oil

Chop the scallions and onion very fine. Sauté them in some oil with a little salt until the onions are tender, cooked through, and a little brown on the edges. Set them aside.

Prepare the dough by incorporating the cold water into the flour gradually. You may have to adjust the exact amount of water needed. The dough must be strong and smooth. Knead it well.

Turn the dough out onto the counter or cutting board. Don't add extra flour to the surface for rolling. Roll out the entire mass of dough to a rectangle, about 24 by 30 inches and $3/8$ inch thick.

Indent the dough with your finger tips, and spread the cooked scallions and oil evenly over the surface. Sprinkle a dusting of flour, salt, and Five Spice powder if you like.

Roll the rectangle into a log from the wide end. Cut the roll into sections about 2 inches wide. Each of these will become a large pancake.

Pick up each section, pinching each end with both hands, and quickly twist and compress it into a circle. This forms layers of dough and onion. Roll each section out into a larger circle, 8 to 10 inches across.

Fry the pancakes in a small but ample amount of oil, about five minutes to a side. Flip them once, but move them frequently in a circular motion to prevent them from burning. Cover the pan while the first side is cooking so they cook through.

Stack the pancakes neatly on a large platter and keep them covered with a clean cloth or paper towel to stay hot. The stack may be cut in quarters, making many delicious triangular pieces.

Serve with soy sauce and fresh ginger condiment, or hot chili sauce.

RICE
Dey

1 CUP DRY RICE SERVES 2

Most everyone enjoys rice, and it is a well known staple food. If you serve rice often, or plan to include it in a meal for guests, we recommend Elephant Brand, jasmine rice from Thailand. The rice found in most supermarkets becomes too soft and pasty and has little flavor. Thai jasmine rice is readily available in many shops that sell Oriental foods as it is quite popular. Another favorite is Basmati rice, which comes from India and has a very distinctive and pleasing aroma.

Rice is served with many of the dishes in this book. In most American restaurants rice is served as a side dish, and the portion is often about three quarters of a cup of cooked rice. This is not the portion size that is common to Tibetan meals. The rice is the base of the meal, easily one and one half full cups of cooked rice for the modest eater. The other foods are added to this in lesser quantity.

Electric rice cookers are as common in Tibetan kitchens as toasters are here in America. They can be found in most kitchen supply shops in various sizes. If you cook rice everyday, they are good thing to have and they take the speculation out of the rice cooking process.

Method:

The basic proportion of water to rice is two to one. Whatever the quantity, use the same cup to measure the rice and the water and it will be fine. One cup of dry rice yields about two cups of cooked rice.

If you are cooking rice in a pot, put the rice and cold water in the pot and bring it to a full boil, uncovered. Then cover the pot and turn off the heat. The rice will absorb the water and steam and be done in 15 to 20 minutes.

If using a rice cooker, put the rice and cold water in, cover, and turn it on. The rice will cook, and stay warm, and you will not have to watch it.

BUCKWHEAT PORRIDGE
Diro

I CUP DRY 'DIRO' PER PERSON

Gala was reminded of diro by 'Wheatena' one morning. He described it as a "very dark one" cooked in a pot. I knew it had to be a grain of some kind, and after a little more talk, I went to look in the health food store and found that buckwheat flour fit the description best. Indeed, it was the right stuff, and this staple food, commonly eaten in Nepal, could now become a regular part of the menu at home.

This dish is made without measuring and requires a strong arm and good wooden spoon.

INGREDIENTS:

> **water**
> **oil (olive, peanut, or sesame)**
> **buckwheat flour**

Put water into a pot, equal to the amount of diro you want to make. (A person can eat about 1 to 1½ cups of cooked diro.) Bring the water to a full boil. Add a large dash of oil.

Swiftly pour some buckwheat flour into the water, stirring immediately and vigorously to incorporate the flour into the water. Continue to add buckwheat flour and stir until you have a smooth, thick paste that is clinging to the pot and spoon. Lower the heat and mix continuously, kneading it with the spoon to get out any dry lumps of flour. The diro will sputter and pop, and steam will escape during the process, which should go on for about 10 minutes. The smell of the cooked grain will begin to arise, and as it cooks it will become more elastic.

Turn off the heat and cover, letting it sit for 2 minutes or so.

Diro may be served as a side dish with chicken curry, but it is filling enough to be the main part of a meal that consists of diro surrounded by a thin and spicy soup. Diro is normally eaten with the fingers.

QUICK STEAMED BREAD
Cyokpo Palep Lugpa

SERVES 4

This bread can be made quickly and easily in the simplest of kitchens, including an outdoor fire.

INGREDIENTS:

> 6 cups unbleached white flour
> 4 teaspoons baking powder
> ½ teaspoon baking soda
> 2 cups cold water (approximately)
> oil

Thoroughly mix the baking powder and baking soda into the flour. Slowly add cold water to the center, mixing to form a soft dough. Let the dough sit, covered, for 15 minutes.

Divide the dough into four sections by cutting it in half twice. Shape each section gently with your hands as if forming a snow ball.

Pour ¼ inch of oil in a large stock pot. Arrange the four rounds in the bottom of the pot next to each other. Cover it and turn the flame on low. After a few minutes, check to see if the bread has toasted on the bottom.

Toss in ½ cup cold water and quickly cover to trap the steam. Be careful doing this!

Steam for an additional ten minutes. The water will evaporate and the breads should rise.

Any meal of light soup will be complemented by this bread.

FLATBREAD
Khamba Roti

SERVES 4

Roti, also called chapatti, are simple breads made on the top of the stove or in the fire. They are about 6 inches across, and are served with curries and other wet foods. The best ones are made from dough that has been kneaded extensively to release the gluten. Few of us are conditioned to this level of exercise, so we have devised an adapted version. The result is very edible, and suitable for a breakfast with hard boiled eggs and the chili sauce called martza, or alongside any main dish.

INGREDIENTS:

> 5 cups unbleached white flour
> 1 cup whole wheat flour
> 2 teaspoons baking powder
> water
> oil or butter

Blend the two flours and baking powder together in a mixing bowl. Gradually incorporate cold water, working from the center, until you have a cohesive, pliable dough. Cover and let it rest 15 minutes.

Lightly flour your working surface. Pull off a small handful of dough, rolling it between your palms so that it has no seams. Press it onto the floured surface and roll it out into a circle, approximately 6 to 8 inches across and about ¼ inch thick.

Preheat a cast iron skillet. If you are working alone, make 2 roti before you begin to cook them. You may then get a steady flow of rolled out and cooking roti going to save time. It is also a good idea to use two skillets.

Put 1 teaspoon of oil or butter on the skillet and immediately place the roti on top, rotating it with your fingers. Be sure the heat is not too high, but it must be hot enough to cook quickly. Sections of the roti will begin to puff and fill with air. When this happens, and it is slightly browned, flip it over and cook the other side. Keep it moving.

Use tongs or a spatula to place the cooked roti on a plate or basket covered with a cloth, where it will remain hot until served.

CRISPY RICE
Dey Yeu

(NO SERVING SIZE)

This snack food is long lasting and versatile. Once it is made it can be flavored in small quantities—sweet, salty, or hot—depending on the taste of your guests. It is the Asian version of potato chips or popcorn: inexpensive, easy to prepare, and healthy.

INGREDIENTS:

> 4 cups rice
> water
> butter or oil (peanut or olive oil)

Soak four cups of rice overnight in enough warm water to cover it.

Drain the rice. Heat a heavy skillet and barely coat the bottom with oil or butter when the pan is hot. Add the drained rice and stir continuously with wooden chop sticks. The rice must be moved so that the water evaporates and it browns evenly. When all the rice is nicely brown, it will smell cooked.

Remove the rice from the hot pan and allow it to cool as quickly as possible. This is easy to do if you spread it out on a paper bag, or place it in a large bowl and stir so the steam escapes.

When the rice is cooled it should be stored in a tin. You may add 2 teaspoons of sugar, with a sprinkle of cinnamon, cardamom, and ginger; or salt with a pinch of cayenne, lemon pepper, or curry powder. Even plain, it offers a satisfying crunch and the subtle taste of roasted rice.

Main Dishes

STEAMED DUMPLINGS
Momo

SERVES 4 TO 6

Momos are a well known Tibetan dish that has relatives in many cultures. While it is a laborious process for a single cook to make a large batch, a few skilled momo makers can turn out dozens in an hour. These dumplings are generally served as the main dish, accompanied by condiments.

INGREDIENTS:

> **Dough:**
> 4 cups unbleached white flour
> ½ cups whole wheat flour
> 1 cup cold water

Begin by making the dough. Put both the whole wheat flour and white flour in a large bowl. Gradually add the cold water to the center, mixing by hand until the dough forms. It will be firm, not sticky, and will require considerable muscle to continue kneading for approximately 5 minutes. Let the dough rest, covered, for 15 to 20 minutes while you prepare the filling.

BEEF FILLING
INGREDIENTS:

> 1 pound ground steak
> ½ bunch cilantro (½ cup chopped)
> ½ cube beef bouillon
> 1 bunch scallions (1 cup chopped)
> salt
> soy sauce

Place the ground meat in a bowl. Chop both the cilantro and scallions very fine. Add them to the meat, mixing very well with a spoon.

Dissolve the bouillon in ¾ cup of hot water. Add this to the mixture, stirring well as the texture becomes somewhat soft and smooth. Add salt and soy sauce to taste.

TOFU AND GREEN BEAN FILLING

INGREDIENTS:

> 1 large block tofu
> 6 scallions
> 2 cloves garlic
> 1-inch piece of fresh ginger
> 1 package bean thread noodles (ping)
> 6 mushrooms
> 1 handful string beans
> ½ cup peanut oil
> soy sauce
> 1 teaspoon cornstarch
> 1 cup water

Soak the noodles in very hot water. Parboil the string beans.

Finely chop the scallions, garlic, ginger, mushrooms, string beans, and noodles.

Drain the water out of the tofu by mashing it up in a wok or frying pan over high heat. The water will sizzle right out of it. When it is dry and crumbling add the finely chopped ginger, garlic, mushrooms, soy sauce, and oil. Sauté the mixture for a few minutes before adding the string beans, scallions, and noodles. Cook for a few moments so the flavors blend together.

In a small bowl, stir the cornstarch into the water. Toss it into the tofu mixture and stir till the mixture holds together. Remove from heat and cool.

POTATO FILLING

INGREDIENTS:

5 potatoes
1 onion
½ bunch cilantro (½ cup chopped)
½ bunch scallions (½ cup chopped)
4 tablespoons frozen peas
¼ cup sweet butter
1 teaspoon salt

Peel and wash the potatoes, and cut them into eighths. Place them in a pot of water and boil.

While the potatoes are cooking chop the onion, cilantro, and scallions very fine. Sauté the onion in the butter until it is cooked through. When the potatoes are very soft, drain off the water and mash them. Add them to the cooked onion, along with the cilantro, peas, and scallions. Salt to taste. Allow the filling to cool before using.

CABBAGE FILLING

INGREDIENTS:

1 small green cabbage
1 large onion
3 cloves garlic
1 teaspoon ginger
2 carrots
1 teaspoon cornstarch
3 tablespoons soy sauce
¼ teaspoon cayenne
oil

Grate the carrots and cook for 2 minutes in rapidly boiling water. Drain and set aside.

Chop the cabbage, onion, garlic, and ginger very fine and sauté together with the cayenne in some olive oil until tender. Before removing from the heat, dissolve the cornstarch and soy sauce in 1 cup of cold water. Stir this mixture into the filling and add the cooked carrots.

Allow the mixture to cool before using. (This process can be accelerated by putting it into the freezer and stirring occasionally.)

MUSHROOM AND CHEESE FILLING

INGREDIENTS:

I pound fresh mushrooms
6 dried mushrooms
I large onion
2 cloves garlic
I tablespoon ginger
¼ cup soy sauce
½ bunch scallions (½ cup chopped)
I 8-ounce package cream cheese
½ cup bread crumbs
oil

Soak the dried mushrooms until they become soft.

Chop the fresh mushrooms, onion, garlic, and ginger, and sauté them all together. While these are cooking, chop the dried mushrooms and add them to the mixture along with the soy sauce.

After simmering for a few minutes, remove from the heat and add the cream cheese and bread crumbs, mixing thoroughly. Allow the mixture to cool before using.

FORMING AND COOKING MOMOS

When the filling is made, it is time to roll the dough. It should be quite thin. The traditional method is to roll the dough by hand into a long piece, like making a snake out of clay. One-inch pieces are then broken off and rolled out quite thin with a small rolling pin, one by one. By rolling from the outside edge inward, the center becomes thicker and the edges thinner, which aids in shaping the momos.

Another method for making the circles of dough is perhaps easier: Cut the ball of dough in 4 parts and roll each out as you would a pie crust. You will then have a large sheet of dough, ideally an eighth inch thick. Cut circles of dough using a round cookie cutter or a glass about 3 inches in diameter. A little larger is fine, but smaller is not.

Place all your circles on a lightly floured plate, so they will not stick together, and you are ready to assemble the momos. You will also need a small saucer with a little oil in it.

Pick up one of the circles. Begin by pinching all around the edge to make it a little thinner.

While holding the circle in your left palm, place a teaspoon of filling in the center. With your right hand, pinch the edge in one spot on the right side. Continue to pinch, working your way around the circle and gathering up the edge of the momo until it forms a ball. Make sure the momos are closed well so the juice of the ingredients is sealed inside.

This round shape is one of the common forms. Another is the 'moon' shape. For the moon shape, hold the circle in your left hand and place a teaspoon of filling in the center. With your right hand, fold the circle in half over the filling, and pinch it closed. Fold in and pinch each corner, then pinch closed on either side, shaping a crescent.

When each momo is formed, dip the bottom lightly in the oil and place it in the steamer. The momos should not touch each other. They expand while cooking, and will break if they stick together.

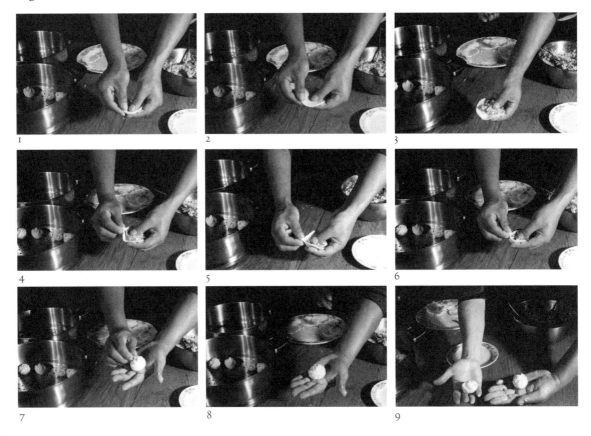

1

2

3

4

5

6

7

8

9

Tibetan Cooking

POTATO AND BEEF
Shogo Tsey

SERVES 6

This is a simple and hearty dish that is easily adjusted to the number of people at hand. Although there is beef in this dish, the potato is the main feature.

INGREDIENTS:

8 large potatoes (any variety)
¾ to 1 pound beef (chuck or sirloin is best)
2 medium onions
2 plum tomato
olive oil
¼ teaspoon turmeric
1 teaspoon salt
1 teaspoon lemon pepper
water

Peel and wash the potatoes, cutting them into 1½ inch pieces. Cut the onions and tomatoes fine, and begin to sauté them in olive oil in a large 8-quart stock pot.

When the onions are tender, toss in the potatoes and spices and stir them around to coat with the onion. Add ½ cup cold water swiftly to the pot and cover, turning down the heat.

Cut the beef into small even pieces. Add this to the cooking potatoes. Add another ½ cup cold water if the potatoes are sticking, and mix thoroughly. Cover and cook over low heat for about 15 minutes. The potatoes should be cooked through but not falling apart.

This dish can be served as a main course with rice, egg soup and chili sauce, or as a side dish when making a larger meal.

SPICY CHICKEN
Chatsey Khatsa

SERVES 6 TO 8

This dish is another great one-pot meal that is served with rice or timo.

INGREDIENTS:

1 whole chicken
2 large onions
6 plum tomatoes
5 cloves garlic
3 tablespoons ginger
2 hot chili peppers
1 sweet red pepper
1 bunch fresh cilantro (1 cup finely chopped)
1 cup frozen peas
1 bunch scallions (1 cup finely chopped)
cayenne
ground black pepper
salt
oil

Take the skin off the chicken and cut up all the parts into 1-inch and 2-inch pieces. Use a meat cleaver so that many pieces have some bone in them. Wash and set aside.

Chop the ginger, chilies, and garlic fine. Cut the onion, tomato, and sweet red pepper in thin slices. Sauté all these vegetables together in enough oil to cover the bottom of a large stock pot.

When the onions begin to cook through, add in the chicken and spices, stirring vigorously to sear.

Continue to cook and stir for 5 minutes or so, then turn down the heat to low and add 1 cup of water. Cover the pot.

Cook slowly for 30 minutes, checking frequently to be sure the food is not burning on the bottom. Add the scallions and peas and continue cooking for 5 minutes more.

The chicken will be tender, falling off the bones, and the vegetables will have become a spicy sauce.

PORK WITH TOFU AND NAPA CABBAGE
Pak Tsey

SERVES 6

This dish can carry the meal or be served as a side. Not all Tibetans eat pork, but those who do love it. This dish is quickly and easily prepared.

INGREDIENTS:

>   6 leaves of Napa cabbage
>   4 boneless pork chops
>   1 block firm tofu
>   3 plum tomatoes
>   2 tablespoons ginger
>   1 onion
>   salt
>   soy sauce
>   1 teaspoon cornstarch
>   water
>   oil

Cut the Napa cabbage, pork, and tofu into 2-inch long, thin rectangles. Leave any fat that is on the pork.

Chop the onion, ginger, and tomato fine and sauté them in a little olive oil. When they are beginning to simmer, add the pork and continue sautéing until it browns.

Add the tofu and some soy sauce and continue to fry, mixing everything together. After about 10 minutes, add the Napa cabbage on top and toss in 1 cup of cold water, into which the cornstarch has been dissolved. Quickly cover the pan, turning down the heat to low. Allow the cabbage to steam for 5 to 7 minutes.

Gently mix the ingredients together and serve steaming hot over rice.

LAMB CURRY
Luk Sha Tsey

SERVES 8

Both sheep and goat were staples of the Tibetan diet. The slaughter would take place just before winter. Enough meat would be harvested to see the family through the winter and into the spring. Because of the yaks' value as pack animals and producers of both dairy and wool, only a few whose time had come were sacrificed. Lamb is therefore a familiar and acceptable meat to offer your Tibetan guests.
Although the use of many spices is still uncommon in many parts of Tibet today, the Tibetans who have grown up exiled in India and Nepal have become accustomed to, and quite like, a very hot curry.

INGREDIENTS:

1 shank of lamb
4 onions
6 cloves garlic
3 tablespoons ginger
6 plum tomatoes
1 cup finely chopped coriander
1 teaspoon salt
3 teaspoons hot curry powder
1 pound fresh spinach
1 cup frozen peas

This meal is cooked in one large 10-quart pot. It is easiest to prepare all ingredients before cooking. Cut all the meat off the shank bone into 1-inch square pieces. (Save the bone to make soup another time, or cook it along with the curry to be eaten later.) Chop the onion and tomato coarsely. Finely chop the garlic, ginger, and coriander.

Sauté all these ingredients in some olive oil, searing the meat, for about 10 minutes. The onions and tomato should begin to form a sauce.

Add the salt, spices, and 1 cup of cold water. Stir well, then turn down the heat and simmer covered for 20 minutes.

Check the meat for doneness, and add the chopped fresh spinach and frozen peas. Simmer for an additional 10 minutes.

Rice or timo is all that is needed to accompany this meal.

BOILED MEAT
Sha Tse Fok

SERVES 4

When I first learned that boiled meat was a favorite dish of Tibetans, I thought I was being teased. This was directly opposite to the French approach to cooking meat I was accustomed to, and it was hard to imagine what there was to enjoy in such a dish. I soon learned that this was a very simple way to have meat on hand for unexpected welcome guests, and as a great, tasty protein snack.

It is very easy to prepare in any quantity, and most of the fat is eliminated through this method. The most important element is the selection of the meat. The preferred cut is chuck with bones or short ribs. Having bones is very important both for the resulting soup stock and the enjoyment and health benefit of chewing on the bones and marrow.

INGREDIENTS:

> 2 to 4 bone-in chuck steaks
> I beef bouillon cube
> I tablespoon salt
> I tablespoon whole black pepper
> (optional herbs such as bay leaf may also be added)

Cut the steaks into 2 or 3 pieces along the bones, and leave the ribs whole. Place the meat in a large stock pot and add cold water to cover it. Add the salt and seasonings and bring it to a boil on high heat. When boiling, lower the heat slightly and continue to boil until the meat is cooked through. Often brown fat rises to the top, which can be skimmed off and discarded, leaving a clear meat stock.

When the meat is cooked, remove it and place it on a large platter to cool. Save the stock for soups or discard it.

The boiled meat is served on a platter uncut. Have sharp knives, small plates, and napkins available. Each person is free to choose their own piece of meat, and it is eaten by hand. Any meat that is left can be refrigerated and is greatly appreciated served cold, with martza chili sauce (see p. 65) as a snack. Therefore, if you are entertaining a number of Tibetans, you can never boil too much meat.

BITTER MELON AND BEEF
Sha Chin Tsey

SERVES 6

Many of us in the West have never eaten this vegetable but it is very popular among Tibetans. It is commonly available in Asian grocery stores. The vegetable is a young loufa, a member of the gourd family. It is light green in color, 8 to 10 inches long, shaped like a cucumber, and very lumpy. This dish may be served as a main dish with plenty of rice, or as a side dish at a big meal.

INGREDIENTS:

> 3 medium-sized bitter melons
> 1 large onion
> ½ pound steak
> salt
> olive oil

Cut the onion into long slices and begin frying it in oil with a little salt. Wash and cut the bitter melon into ½-inch strips. Similarly, slice the steak into thin strips.

Add the bitter melon to the onion and cook it over medium heat for about 10 minutes. It will begin to soften. Add the steak and continue to stir-fry for another 10 minutes. When the meat is just cooked through and the bitter melon is tender it is ready.

This dish should be served with rice, salt, and chili sauce, followed by yogurt. It is wonderfully bitter, definitely an acquired taste.

DAIKON AND BEEF
Lafu Tsey

SERVES 6

This is a very simple dish, often served with rice as a hearty lunch. You may also serve it as a meat course in a more elaborate meal.

INGREDIENTS:

> 2 pounds London broil
> 1 large daikon
> 1 onion
> 1 tablespoon ginger
> 6 to 8 scallions
> 2 tablespoons soy sauce
> salt
> oil

As with many of the recipes in this book, begin by preparing all the ingredients first. This cuts down on cleaning up and cooking time.

Cut the steak lengthwise into two strips about 2½ inches wide. Slice thinly on an angle, with the grain of the meat. Set aside in a bowl and pour the soy sauce over the top.

Chop the ginger and onion finely. Scrub the daikon and slice it into rectangles a similar size to the meat but a little thicker. Chop the scallions into 1-inch pieces and set aside.

Heat a large frying pan, coat it with oil, and sauté the onion and ginger for 1 or 2 minutes. Add the steak and turn up the heat, tossing to sear the meat for 2 minutes. Add the daikon and sauté for another 2 minutes.

Add a little salt, turn the heat to low, and cover. Simmer for 5 minutes. Turn off the heat and add the scallions. Mix these in and serve.

DRIED MEAT
Sha Khampo

(NO SERVING SIZE)

Meat was most commonly preserved in Tibet by drying, either in the open air or buried in mounds. The high altitude, wind, and cold are perfect natural conditions for this method. The meat becomes very light, and is therefore easily transported in a sack, available for chewing or softening in a cup of butter tea. Having lightweight protein was a necessity for nomadic people, and I am sure it would be appreciated by trekkers today. Dried yak meat is especially delicious and surprisingly tender.

Dried meat can be made at home very easily. The most important element is finding the proper place to dry the meat. At home we use our unfinished attic space above the insulated ceiling, which has open air flowing through the eaves. (We have stapled rows of heavy string between the rafters, and we send our son, who is the best size for working up there, to hang or retrieve the meat.) Any cool building or storage shed that is inaccessible to animals would also be suitable for drying. I have seen meat drying in the sun on rooftops. In the open air, the meat should be covered with cheesecloth or mesh screening to keep flies off. Creating the best set-up for your living situation is the biggest challenge. Once this is accomplished the rest is quite simple.

You can also use an electric food drier. These are equipped with shelves where the meat can be dried in a matter of hours. This is a good method if you have no place for drying, or if you find it strange to have meat hanging in your closet. It also suits our custom of getting things done quickly. An electric food dryer needs a power source and makes some noise, which deters us from using it. Also, a greater quantity can be produced at once with the right drying set-up.

Initially, I had reservations about eating home-made dried meat. But this simple method actually produces a healthier product than commercially processed beef jerky, which often contains many preservatives, fat, and sugar. The healthiest choice is natural beef, which is now commonly available at regular food stores. It should be as fresh as possible. Almost any cut can be used, but we use mainly shoulder London broil and round. What appears to be a large quantity of meat reduces down very significantly when dried, so we always start with a minimum of five pounds of meat to justify the effort.

INGREDIENTS:

> 5 pounds or more of London broil or round steak
> salt
> spices (optional: cayenne pepper, coriander powder, turmeric, or garam masala)

Slice the meat into thin strips. You may salt and spice it lightly. We recommend cayenne pepper, coriander powder, turmeric, or garam masala used sparingly. Layer the strips on a tray, and lightly salt or sprinkle a salt and spice mixture on the layers as you go.

Drape the strips over string and leave them to dry. In the summer, the meat is ready in 4 days if you can't wait to try it, but it is better after a week. During winter, check it in 7 to 10 days.

Store the dried meat in plastic food storage bags or cloth bags in a dry place like a kitchen cupboard. It was traditionally stored in a cloth bag, which does not retain moisture and allows the meat to continue drying. You can make one out of muslin, or save a burlap bag from basmati rice for this purpose.

I have also seen another method of making dried meat, where the meat is first cut into small rectangles and boiled. It is then dried on cloth or paper in the open air, or in a cupboard. I prefer the first method. The resulting product looks more palatable and retains more nutrients.

You may offer dried meat at any time your guests are hungry. You can pass the bag around or place a quantity on a serving tray. Accompanied by a hot cup of Tibetan tea, you will be transported to the Tibetan plateau.

KHAMBA PIE
Tab Dey

SERVES 4 TO 6

Upon returning home at lunchtime one day, I was surprised to find the house smelling delicious, with two of my favorite Tibetans standing next to the pot grinning. "We made this one," they told me. "This one is good at animal-watching time."

I was allowed to look into the pot and saw an extraordinary stew cooking inside a shell of Tibetan bread. This is another one-pot dish that can be cooked anywhere, using any meat and vegetables that are at hand.

INGREDIENTS:

Dough:
6 cups unbleached white flour
4 teaspoons baking powder
cold water
¼ teaspoon salt

Filling:
1 pound beef or lamb
4 potatoes
2 tomatoes
3 scallions
6 mushrooms
1 tablespoon soy sauce
½ teaspoon salt
1 cup water
½ cup oil

Mix the flour, baking powder, water, and salt into a firm dough. Set it aside to rest.

While the dough is resting, cut the meat and vegetables into small pieces of uniform size.

Roll the dough into a large circle about ½ inch thick. If you do not have a rolling pin and board, shape the circle with your hands like a pizza.

Warm a pot on medium heat and then pour in the oil, swirling it around to coat the sides. Fit the dough into the pot like a lining, pressing it down at the bottom and up around the sides. The oil should enable the crust to brown and prevent the dough from sticking to the sides of the pot.

Put the meat and vegetables inside the dough lining, with the water, soy sauce, and salt. Cover and cook over low heat for 30 minutes. The bread and stew steam together and are then eaten together by hand.

EGG CURRY
Gonga Tsey

SERVES 2 TO 4

This dish is a great short-notice lunch. It stands on its own served with rice, and looks good too.

INGREDIENTS:

6 eggs
1 large onion
3 cloves garlic
1 to 3 large fresh tomatoes (or 1 cup canned tomato puree)
1 tablespoon fresh ginger
¼ teaspoon salt
2 teaspoons curry powder
olive oil
¼ to ½ cup frozen peas
2 to 3 scallions

Place 6 eggs in a pot and hard boil (cook at boiling point for 10 minutes). Slice the onion and tomato. Finely chop the garlic and ginger.

Using a large cast iron frying pan, just cover the surface with olive oil. Fry the onion, and add the garlic, ginger, tomato, and salt in that order, stirring constantly. Lower the heat, cover the pan, and simmer for 10 to 15 minutes.

While the curry sauce is cooking, peel the hard boiled eggs and slice them in half. Arrange the eggs with the yolk side up in the frying pan. Sprinkle in the frozen peas and scallions. Cover and simmer over very low heat for another 5 minutes.

The result is a colorful tasty dish that may be placed on the table directly in the frying pan.

Vegetarian Dishes

BOK CHOY with TOFU
Petse Tofu

SERVES 4

This is a simple vegetarian dish, bland and watery, that may be served as a main dish over rice, or as a complement to a main course of beef.

INGREDIENTS:

 2 blocks firm tofu (16 oz. each)
 1 large onion
 2 cloves garlic
 1 tablespoon ginger
 5 stalks of bok choy
 3 tablespoons soy sauce
 1 teaspoon cornstarch
 1½ cups cold water
 olive or sesame oil

Chop the garlic and ginger very fine and set aside. Slice the onion thinly. Cut the tofu into ½-inch by 2-inch triangles and set aside to drain. Cut the bok choy into 2-inch triangles.

Coat a deep skillet with ¼ inch of oil and sauté the garlic, ginger, and onion. When the aroma of onion arises, add the tofu and sauté until it browns slightly at the edges.

In a small bowl, dissolve the cornstarch and soy sauce into the cold water.

Add the bok choy to the pan, placing it evenly on top of the sautéed tofu, and quickly pour the cornstarch mixture over it. Cover and turn the heat to low. Simmer for 10 minutes.

Stir gently and serve.

THREE FRIENDS
Ping Sa

SERVES 6

This dish can be served as a main dish in a vegetarian meal with the addition of bread or grain. Mushrooms dominate the dish, so it would be perfect to serve when meat-eaters are in the minority at the table, and they will still feel satisfied with the meal.

INGREDIENTS:

30 dried shiitake mushrooms
3 cloves garlic
2 tablespoons ginger
1 small onion
2 large sweet red peppers
1½ pounds fresh snow peas
oil
salt or soy sauce
1 teaspoon cornstarch
1½ cups water

Wash the mushrooms quickly with very hot water. Place them in a covered bowl with hot water to soften for 1 hour. Remove the stems before cooking.

Finely chop the garlic, ginger, and onion, setting them aside in one bowl. Wash and remove the seeds from the red peppers, and cut them into 1½-inch pieces. Wash the snow peas, removing any large stems.

Put ¼ inch of oil into a skillet and fry the onion, garlic, and ginger over a medium flame. Add a little salt to bring the water out of the onion. When the onion is transparent, add the red peppers, stirring continuously. After 1 or 2 minutes, add the mushrooms and ½ cup of water. Turn the heat down and cover.

Simmer for 5 minutes. Dissolve the cornstarch in 1 cup of water, and add 2 tablespoons of soy sauce. Add this to the pan along with the snow peas. Cover and simmer for 5 minutes.

The dish will be colorful, red and green and shiny.

GOOD POTATOES
Shogo Shimbu Du

SERVES 6

Potatoes are a favored vegetable among Tibetans. This is a good way to prepare them as a side dish.

INGREDIENTS:

8 potatoes
four plum tomatoes
2 small onions
2 cloves garlic
½ teaspoon salt
½ teaspoon black pepper
½ cup finely chopped coriander (or ½ teaspoon ground coriander seed)
½ teaspoon turmeric
olive oil
2 scallions, finely chopped

Peel the potatoes, wash and cut them into 1-inch pieces. Boil them until tender.

Dice the onions, garlic, and tomatoes. Sauté them in a little olive oil, adding salt, pepper, coriander, and turmeric. Cook over low heat, adding a little water if the tomatoes begin to stick.

When the potatoes are done, drain them. Put both the potatoes and the tomato mixture into a large serving bowl and gently toss. Garnish with finely chopped scallions.

POTATO CAKES
Shogo Cake

SERVES 4

These make a good light meal with a little yogurt or green vegetables. They may also be served as an interesting side dish if you are preparing a meal with many dishes. The grating can be done by hand, or you can use a food processor.

INGREDIENTS:

3 large potatoes
1 medium-sized onion
2 eggs
½ cup flour
½ teaspoon baking powder
salt
pepper
oil

Peel and wash the potatoes. Using the large grid, grate the potatoes and onions into a mixing bowl. Add the eggs, blending them in with a fork.

Measure the flour and mix in the baking powder, adding a dash of salt and pepper. Incorporate the flour mixture into the potato mixture.

Heat a frying pan and pour in about ¼ inch oil for frying. (I generally use olive oil for its taste and food value.) Spoon the potato mixture into the pan in rounds about 4 inches in diameter and ¾ inch thick. Keep the heat medium to low so the cakes don't burn. The edges will begin to brown in about 5 minutes. Turn with a spatula and cook on the other side. Cook them to a golden brown, crispy on the outside, and soft in the center. This takes about 15 to 20 minutes.

Most people enjoy potatoes. This dish looks good, and although it is a universal recipe, it becomes Asian when served with achar (see p.61) and yogurt.

DRIED MUSHROOMS WITH TOFU AND BEAN THREAD NOODLES
Shimong Khampo

SERVES 6

This dish may be served as a main course or a side dish. If you cultivate the habit of storing dried goods, you may have the bean threads and mushrooms in your cupboard. It then becomes possible to present this somewhat exotic dish on short notice.

Mushrooms are considered a substitute for meat. With the protein from the tofu, this makes a good vegetarian main dish that non-vegetarians can enjoy.

INGREDIENTS:

3 packages dried bean thread noodles (ping)
24 dried shiitake mushrooms
2 blocks silken tofu
3 plum tomatoes
1 tablespoon ginger
2 cloves garlic
1 small onion
olive oil
¼ cup soy sauce
1 cup water
1 teaspoon cornstarch

First rinse the mushrooms, then soak them in very hot water for at least 25 minutes. (They may also be boiled to hasten the softening, or left to soak in water overnight.) Place the bean thread noodles in a bowl of very hot water to soften. While these two ingredients are soaking, prepare the rest for cooking.

Slice the garlic, onion, and tomato into thin slivers. Finely chop the ginger and slice the tofu into ½-inch pieces.

Fry the onion, garlic, ginger, and tomato in olive oil in a deep cast iron pan. While these ingredients are cooking, squeeze the water out of the mushrooms and cut off the stems if they are still tough. Once the onions are soft, add the mushrooms and lower the heat. Cover and cook for 5 minutes.

Combine the water, cornstarch, and soy sauce. Add the tofu to the mushrooms, then pour in the cornstarch mixture. Cover and continue to cook over low heat for another 5 minutes. Be careful not to burn it. Use a spatula to mix the tofu and mushrooms gently to assure even cooking.

Cut the bean threads in half and add to the pan. (You will find that scissors work best for this.) Sprinkle with soy sauce and an additional ½ cup of water. Cover and simmer on low heat for 5 minutes.

The slow cooking and addition of soy sauce release the flavor of the mushrooms which dominates the dish. If you are serving this to people who enjoy very hot food, a ½ teaspoon of red cayenne pepper may be added at the beginning. This will give the dish a suggestion of hotness.

Serve with rice or timo on the side.

Variation: Add 2 long hot peppers, thinly sliced, when sautéing the garlic and onion. This will add color and heat and will particularly please Tibetan taste buds.

TOFU "CHICKEN"
Tofu Chatsey

SERVES 6

Vegetarians will especially appreciate this dish. It is best served with rice and a vegetable side dish, such as Green Cabbage (p. 43) or String beans with Garlic (p. 45) for a completely satisfying meal.

INGREDIENTS:

> 2 pounds firm tofu
> 2 tablespoons soy sauce
> I teaspoon garlic powder
> I cup water
> 2 eggs
> ½ cup cornstarch
> oil

The secret to this dish lies in freezing and thawing the tofu to change its texture. When you buy the tofu, place it in the freezer instead of the refrigerator. Before making the dish, thaw the tofu by leaving it out for 5 hours or so. You can speed the thawing by defrosting it in the microwave or placing it in very hot water.

Squeeze all the water out of the tofu by pressing it gently between your hands. You will now a have a tofu sponge. Allow it to sit and continue to drain while you prepare the other ingredients.

Use a wire whisk to blend the water, soy sauce, garlic powder, and eggs in a small mixing bowl.

Put the cornstarch onto a flat plate. Cut the tofu and place it on another plate. You must work carefully as it is very crumbly and it is nice to have evenly sized pieces. Make them a little large.

Heat about ½ inch oil in a deep frying pan. Arrange the cornstarch, egg mixture, and tofu beside the pan in that order, with the cornstarch closest to the pan. Using chop sticks or two forks, and being careful not to break the tofu, dip it first in the egg, which it will absorb quickly. Then roll it in cornstarch and fry gently until crisp.

Remove to a plate covered with a paper towel to absorb the excess oil. That's it! Garnish with some bright greens such as water cress or cilantro. Salad is also a great companion for this dish.

GREEN CABBAGE
Tsong Jangu

SERVES 6

Green cabbage is a commonly prepared vegetable in Nepal. It is most often used to fill out a dish. This recipe is a light and flavorful treatment that is digestible and gives cabbage its own place at the table.

INGREDIENTS:

- 1 green cabbage (6-inch diameter)
- 1 medium-sized onion
- 3 cloves garlic
- 2 tablespoons ginger
- 2 teaspoons soy sauce
- ¾ cup water
- 1 teaspoon cornstarch
- 1 teaspoon sesame oil
- oil

Cut the cabbage into 3-inch triangles. Rinse them with cold water and let them drain.

Finely chop the onion, garlic, and ginger. Preheat a deep skillet, coat it with oil and sauté the onion, garlic, and ginger for about 2 minutes. Then add the cabbage, stirring to mix with the oil and seasonings.

Add the sesame oil, turn down the heat, and cover the pan for another 2 or 3 minutes.

Mix together the water, soy sauce, and cornstarch. Stir this mixture into the cabbage, cover, and cook for another 2 minutes over low heat. The cabbage should be cooked through and tender while retaining its shape.

If your guests are fond of spicy food, it is very simple to substitute hot sesame oil which greatly enhances the flavor of this dish.

GALA'S GRILLED MUSHROOMS
Shimong Sak Cho

SERVES 4   SERVING SIZE: APPROX ¼ LB. PER PERSON

This is a great way to cook mushrooms quickly that both preserves and enhances their unique form and flavor.

INGREDIENTS:

> 1 pound fresh mushrooms
> 1 tablespoon oil
> salt
> ½ cup beef or vegetable stock
> butter (optional)

Clean the mushrooms and remove the stems.

Place a large cast iron skillet on the stove over high heat. Lightly coat the pan with olive oil and place the mushrooms in one layer, top side down. After a few minutes of cooking sprinkle them with salt. The salt will cause the natural water inside the mushroom to collect in the center where the stem used to be.

When the mushrooms begin to darken, quickly pour in the beef stock and cover, turning down the heat. Allow to simmer for 3 minutes, or until done.

The original version of this recipe is to cook the mushrooms on an outdoor grill. No pan is needed. Just place the mushrooms on the grill, top side down, and salt them. The salt draws the water out of the mushroom to form a small pool. They taste wonderful flavored by the smoke.

STRING BEANS WITH GARLIC
Gok Tse

SERVES 6

This is a tasty and nutritious side dish that is easy to prepare, and is a colorful complement to almost any meal.

INGREDIENTS:

> 2 pounds fresh string beans
> 10 cloves garlic
> 3 tablespoons butter
> oil
> salt
> soy sauce
> ¼ cup water

Break the stems and tail ends off the beans. Wash them in cold water and let them stand in a colander to drain.

Slice the garlic cloves into thin slivers. Melt the butter in a cast iron pan and sauté the garlic lightly for about 1 minute. Then add oil to cover the pan.

When the garlic releases its fragrance add a sprinkle of salt and the soy sauce, stirring continuously. Be careful not to burn the garlic.

Have ¼ cup cold water ready. Add the string beans, tossing them together with the garlic and oil. Quickly add the water and cover the pan to trap the steam.

Turn the heat down low and simmer for 5 to 7 minutes.

The string beans should be hot and tender, but still very green and not over-cooked.

STEAMED GREENS
Ngo Tse

The word is out among Tibetans everywhere that eating greens is good for you—even for Tibetan people. I have met Tibetans that enjoy salad, but it would not be on the top ten list of favorite dishes. Steamed greens is a good way to bring greens into a meal.

They blend well with rice and meat dishes, and will be enjoyed whether bland, bitter, or spicy.

Rather than an exact recipe, these are quick and easy methods for preparing all sorts of greens. The following fresh vegetables make good sides of green. Buy organic whenever possible.

Spinach	Beet greens	Broccoli rabe
Kale	Turnip greens	Mustard greens
Chard	Baby bok choy	Dandelion
Escarole	Endive	

Before cooking greens by your chosen method, take these simple steps:

· Wash the greens thoroughly

· Cut off any tough stems, ends, or rotted spots

· With the exception of spinach, chop the greens finely and set in a colander to drain

STEAMED, PLAIN

Place the greens in a steamer, and steam until tender. There are pots that have a steaming basket which fits inside the larger pot, so while you are boiling potatoes or meat, the greens can be steamed at the same time. You may serve them as is, or dress with a little butter or olive oil and salt. The taste of the greens will not be enhanced or disguised in any way.

STEAMED WITH SEASONING

Place the greens in the steamer along with fresh or dried herbs, such as coriander, cumin, fennel or oregano. A touch of cayenne paper will make the greens hot. I usually have it available on the side. The herbs add their subtle taste and fragrance.

SAUTÉED

Select a frying pan with a tight-fitting lid. Sauté a small amount of garlic, onion, or ginger, or all three, in just enough oil to coat the pan. When the onion turns clear, pile in the greens and toss them around. The greens will begin to wilt and reduce in bulk immediately. When the sautéed ingredients and the greens are mixed together well, toss in at least ½ cup of cold water and 1 tablespoon of soy sauce, covering the frying pan immediately. Turn the gas down to low and steam slowly for about 7 minutes until done. If you want the greens to be spicy, sprinkle in some cayenne pepper before you add the water and soy sauce.

You may enjoy the bitter earthy taste of greens, as many Tibetans do. The leftovers can be used in soups, or served cold with oil and vinegar as a cooked salad. They always look good on the table, too.

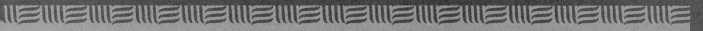

Soups

RICE SOUP
Dey Tuk

SERVES 2 TO 4

This soup is a good breakfast food for cold winter mornings. It is also suitable for babies or people who are not feeling well. Dey tuk is essentially a method of making a little cooked rice go a long way, and is a naturally bland base for variations to suit the taste of those being served. It is very easy to digest.

INGREDIENTS:

    1 cup cooked rice
    4 cups water

    Optional additions:
    milk, half-and-half, butter, sugar, maple syrup
    salt, soy sauce, beef bouillon
    finely chopped beef
    finely chopped scallions
    freshly grated ginger

Put the rice and cold water into a saucepan and bring to a boil over medium heat, stirring occasionally to avoid burning the rice. Once the mixture has reached a boil, turn the heat very low and continue stirring. The rice should begin to become soft and glutinous and lose its shape. You may wish to use an egg beater or potato masher to make the soup smooth.

At this point the soup can become a sweet food or an easily digested protein food depending on the ingredients added.

For sweet dey tuk, add 1 cup of milk or half-and-half. Continue to cook over low heat while stirring. Add 1 tablespoon of unsalted butter and sugar, maple syrup, or honey to taste.

For savory dey tuk, you can use only salt or soy sauce, and butter. Or add 1 cup of beef broth or a bouillon cube dissolved in 1 cup of water. Continue to cook over low heat while stirring. Garnish with chopped scallions if desired. Finely chopped meat may also be added and cooked until done.

Served plain, or with minimal additions, dey tuk is a healing comfort food.

DUMPLING SOUP
Mo Tuk

SERVES 4

Mo tuk, a wonderful dish for winter, is the Tibetan version of won-ton soup, though the differences are many. The dumpling is made into a "mouse" shape, and is small, about 2 inches long. Traditionally the filling is seasoned beef, the same as beef momo filling. The soup is made flavorful and thick by boiling the dumplings, and the addition of soft cheese and green onion.

INGREDIENTS:

Dough for dumplings:
4 cups white flour
1 cup water

Filling for dumplings:
1 lb. ground beef
½ bunch fresh cilantro (½ cup chopped)
½ bunch fresh scallions (½ cup chopped)
3 tablespoons oil
½ cup warm water
salt

Broth:
1 beef bouillon cube
2 slices American cheese
6 finely chopped scallions for garnish

Prepare the dough by gradually incorporating the water into the flour. It should be smooth and firm for rolling. Set this aside while you prepare the filling.

In a medium-size mixing bowl, combine the ground beef, cilantro, scallions, oil, and water. These ingredients should be kneaded together by hand so they are well blended and the meat becomes more tender. Add a little salt to taste.

Roll the dough out onto a floured board or counter, to about 1/8 inch thick. Thin, pliable dough is required to form the dumplings. Using a 2½-inch round cookie cutter or glass, make as many circles as possible. Place these on a lightly floured plate.

Have a lightly oiled tray ready to place the dumplings on as they are shaped. Holding a circle of dough in your left hand, place a teaspoon of filling in the center. Crimp one end, then pinch an overlapping fold down the center, and end it with a fine twist or "tail."

When all the dumplings are made, bring the stock to the boiling point. Slide the dumplings into the pot carefully, a few at a time, while stirring. In this way they will not stick and you will not be splashed with the hot soup. The dumplings will be cooked through in about 15 to 20 minutes. You can take one out to test it.

Before serving add a handful of finely chopped scallions to the pot. Serve in small bowls so that guests may have many helpings.

Lunch break at stupa consecration ceremony in Kathmandu

Cooking tent for thousands, vegetarian lunch

Tibetan tea being served in Bodh Gaya

Bok choy with tofu (Petse tofu, p. 36) and scallion pancake (Tsey Paklep, p. 8)

Daikon and beef (Lafu Tsey, p. 29)

Tsampa tossing in hot sand

Sweet tea for five hundred, Kathmandu, Nepal

Torma butter sculpture offerings in Bodh Gaya.

Potato and beef (Shogo Tsey, p. 21) with steamed greens (Ngo Tse, p. 46) and momos (p. 16)

Losar Khapsay

Vegetarian lunch in Swayambhunath, Nepal

Pounding barley for Surprise Soup (Gu Tuk, p. 104)

The author and her dog, Dolma

Sweet bread (Ngamo Palep, p. 3)

Noodle soup (Ten Tuk, p. 54)

WHOLE BARLEY SOUP
Ney Tuk

SERVES 4 AS A MAIN DISH, 6 TO 8 AS AN APPETIZER

INGREDIENTS:

1 cup pearl barley
12 dried black mushrooms
½ pound steak
4 cloves garlic
2 tablespoons fresh ginger
1 beef bouillon cube
a pinch of cayenne pepper (optional)
½ pound spinach

Wash the barley in cold water, and soak in cold water overnight or for at least 1 hour. Wash the mushrooms with hot water, and soak overnight or for at least 1 hour.

Cut the mushrooms into strips and put the barley and mushrooms into a 3 qt. pot with 6 cups of cold water and the bouillon cube. Bring to a boil, then simmer for 30 minutes. The water will gradually cook down, and the gluten in the barley will thicken. Hot water must be added continuously or the soup will become too thick.

Finely chop the garlic and ginger and add to the soup with the olive oil. The cayenne can be eliminated or increased according to your taste. A pinch will give a very slight hotness to the soup and will enhance the flavor. Cook for another 30 minutes or so.

Cut the steak into thin slices, 1 inch long and add them to the soup. Cook only a few minutes so the meat will be tender. Check to see if more water is needed for the consistency.

Add the fresh cut spinach at the end before serving so it will remain bright green and flavorful.

NOODLE SOUP
Ten Tuk

SERVES 6

This is our household favorite. Whatever cannot be eaten at dinner time is quickly consumed for breakfast.

INGREDIENTS:

6 cups unbleached white flour
3½ cups cold water
1 egg (optional)
1 pound beef (sirloin, chuck, or London broil)
2 beef bouillon cubes
1 large onion
2 tablespoons ginger
olive oil
¼ teaspoon cayenne pepper
¼ cup soy sauce
1 pound fresh spinach
4 scallions

First make the dough for the ten tuk noodles: Put the flour in a large bowl. Gradually mix the water in by hand from a well in the center. If you want to add an egg, do so now. The addition of egg makes the noodles firmer, and they absorb less of the broth. The dough should be soft and pliable but not sticky. Set it aside. (I usually turn it onto the floured counter and cover it with the bowl to rest while the soup is being prepared.)

Cut the meat into small pieces, about 1½ inches long and ½ inch thick. Finely chop the onion and ginger.

Sauté the onion and ginger in olive oil. Add the meat and 2 bouillon cubes. Toss these around and turn down the heat, allowing them to simmer for 5 minutes. Then add 4 cups cold water and cover.

Now it is time to shape the noodles. There are numerous techniques for this. The authentic ten tuk shape I learned from my Ama can be made anywhere without the use of a cutting board or rolling pin. If half the people who are going to eat help, the work is done very fast. First oil your clean hands. Pull off a small handful of dough and squeeze it into a snake, making it longer, thinner, and flatter as you go. Repeatedly oil your hands so the dough is easy to work. This oil will end up in the soup.

After all the dough is turned into long strips, bring the soup just to a boil and stir. Add the noodles by swiftly pulling off thumb-size pieces and throwing them directly into the moving soup. When all the noodles are in the soup, continue to cook it for another 15 minutes on low heat.

Just before serving, add the fresh chopped spinach, stir it in, and turn off the heat. Let the ten tuk sit for 2 minutes, then serve. The spinach will be green and beautiful.

This is a complete and very satisfying meal. Offer some hot sauce and salt on the side.

EASY EGG SOUP
Gong Tuk

SERVES 4 TO 6

This soup is good served alongside momos, or as an accompaniment to Boiled or Dried Meat.

INGREDIENTS:

> 8 cups water
> 1 beef bouillon cube
> 4 eggs
> 1 plum tomato
> 10 large leaves of fresh spinach
> pinch of salt
> 1 teaspoon soy sauce

Place the beef bouillon cube in a pot with the water. Bring to a full rolling boil. Slice the tomato thinly.

Whisk the eggs in a bowl, and then toss them quickly into the boiling water. Turn off the heat. Add the spinach leaves, shredding them by hand, and the tomato.

Add salt and soy sauce.

This soup looks very nice with the red and green of the fresh vegetables and has a mild taste.

SALTY TOFU AND SPINACH SOUP
Tsa Tofu Tuk

SERVES 6

This soup is good served with timo. It is a bit salty by Western standards, but satisfying as occasional fare. You can offer rice on the side that may be added to the soup individually. A large bowl is hearty enough to be a vegetarian main course. It is also very economical.

INGREDIENTS:

> ¼ cup olive oil
> 1 16-oz. package of tofu
> 1 large onion
> 1 large tomato
> oil
> 2 vegetable bouillon cubes
> 2 tablespoons soy sauce
> 2 slices American cheese
> 1 can cooked red kidney beans
> 1 pound fresh spinach
> 12 cups of water

Cut the tofu into small ½-inch pieces and set them aside to drain. Finely chop the onion and tomato. Dissolve the bouillon cubes in 1 cup of hot water. Finely chop the fresh spinach.

Sauté the onion and tomato in oil. When the onion is soft, add the soy sauce, dissolved bouillon and 2 more cups of water. Simmer for 5 minutes.

Add the remaining 9 cups of water and bring to a boil. Then add the rest of the ingredients in this order: first the cheese, then the beans, tofu, and lastly the spinach. Stir to blend the ingredients as you add them.

When the soup reaches a boil after these additions, cover it and turn off the heat. Allow the soup to sit for 5 minutes before serving.

SWEET NOODLES
Pa Tuk

SERVES 4 TO 6

This dish is made at the time of the full moon, and is often served as the last meal before the fasting phase of the Nunye practice. It is very filling and is served alone. Pa tuk is a bowl of warm, edible spheres.

INGREDIENTS:

>   8 cups unbleached white flour
>   2 cups cold water (approximately)
>   1 egg
>   ¼ cup butter
>   ½ cup sugar

Break the egg into the center of the flour, and slowly blend in cold water until a dough is formed that is easy to handle, soft but not sticky.

Pull off a handful of dough, and on a floured board roll it into a "snake" about 1 inch in diameter. Then pull off 1-inch pieces and roll in the palm of the hand to form a ball. Keep these from sticking together by rolling them on the lightly floured board. Continue this process until all the dough is used.

Bring an 8-quart saucepan full of water to a rapid boil, and drop the balls in carefully, stirring all the while. Cook over low heat for 15 to 20 minutes, until they are cooked through. They will grow a little bigger in the water.

Drain the pa tuk and add the butter and sugar while it is very hot. A variation is to add butter and granulated, dried yak cheese.

Serve in a small bowl.

Condiments and Dairy

PICKLED SALAD
Tang Tse

SERVES 2 TO 4

This condiment is fresh and crunchy. Its sharp, cool taste complements any spicy dish. It is easy to make and can be refrigerated.

INGREDIENTS:

    1 cucumber
    1 small daikon
    2 carrots
    4 tablespoons vinegar
    ½ teaspoon salt

Peel the cucumber, daikon, and carrots. Cut them all into matchstick pieces, $1/8$ inch thick by 2 inches long.

Combine all three vegetables in a bowl, sprinkling the mixture with salt and vinegar. Let it stand a few minutes before serving in small bowls alongside the main dish.

FRESH TOMATO CHUTNEY
Achar

SERVES 4 TO 8

INGREDIENTS:

4 or 5 fresh tomatoes
1 medium-size onion
1 clove garlic
1 tablespoon ginger
¼ teaspoon cayenne pepper
¼ cup olive oil
½ teaspoon salt

Chop the onion, garlic, and ginger and fry over medium heat in the olive oil until the onion is soft and clear. Be careful not to burn the garlic.

Add the chopped tomato, salt, and cayenne pepper. Turn down the heat very low, cover and cook for about 10 to 12 minutes, stirring occasionally. When the tomatoes are cooked down, turn off the heat and leave the pot covered.

Serve in a bowl alongside momos. The reserve may be refrigerated and reheated.

JALAPENO & BLUE CHEESE
Ema Dar Tsee

SERVES 2 TO 4

This is a Bhutanese recipe, but a favorite condiment among our Tibetan relatives. It is very hot and pungent.

INGREDIENTS:

> 6 fresh jalapeno peppers
> 6 to 8 ounces blue cheese
> 3 tablespoons olive oil

Wash the peppers and cut them in thirds, removing the seeds and stem. Crumble or chop the blue cheese into a bowl or on a cutting board.

Sauté the peppers in olive oil over medium heat for a few minutes until they become tender. Reduce the heat to very low, then add the blue cheese. Continue to stir as the blue cheese melts and continue cooking for a few more minutes. Place in a serving bowl.

This condiment is best served warm or at room temperature so that the blue cheese is soft. It complements any bland food, such as timo or Boiled Meat, and is good with Bitter Melon and Beef.

This condiment can be kept refrigerated.

DIPPING SAUCE

SERVES 2 TO 4

This is very simple to make and goes especially well with vegetarian momos.

INGREDIENTS:

½ cup soy sauce
¼ cup black vinegar (found in Chinese grocery stores, or substitute balsamic or
    red wine vinegar)
¼ cup water
1 tablespoon ginger

Select an attractive, small serving bowl. Combine the soy sauce, vinegar, and water. Grate the ginger and add it to the liquid mixture.

Place a serving spoon in the bowl and the guests may put small amounts on their plate. For more elaborate settings, provide each guest with a portion in a small bowl for dipping alongside the plate.

Store in the refrigerator, preferably in a glass jar. It improves with age.

DAIKON PICKLE
Tsong Lafu

(NO SERVING SIZE)

This pickle has a good pungent taste and a very powerful aroma. It is a savory accompaniment to meat dishes and offers the nutrients of raw vegetables. This recipe makes 2 quart jars.

INGREDIENTS:

> 1 large daikon
> 1 bunch red radishes
> 2 teaspoons Sichuan pepper
> 2 teaspoons whole dried chili
> 4 tablespoons white vinegar
> 1 teaspoon salt
> water

Peel the daikon. Cut it into 3-inch pieces and then into 1/8-inch slices so you have thin rectangles of daikon. Divide these equally between the two jars.

Wash the radishes, remove stems and roots, and cut them across into thin circles. Divide these between the two jars as well.

To each jar, add 1 teaspoon each of Sichuan pepper and dried chili, along with 2 tablespoons of white vinegar and ½ teaspoon salt.

Fill the jars with water, leaving some room at the top to shake the mixture. Place the jars in a sunny window for 3 or 4 days and the pickle will be done. It should then be refrigerated and used within a week. The red from the radishes colors the water and the makes the daikon slightly pink.

This pickle goes well with Boiled Meat.

HOMEMADE CHILI SAUCE
Martza

This extremely hot sauce can be made with ingredients found at any health food store that has dried herbs in bulk. Keeping this on hand allows us to cook mild food and still satisfy those who are accustomed to Asian spices. It is best to prepare this in a small, covered container in which it can be kept and served.

INGREDIENTS:

3 teaspoons very hot cayenne pepper powder (90,000 units)
1 teaspoon mild red pepper
2 teaspoons whole red cayenne pepper
½ teaspoon turmeric
½ teaspoon garlic powder
½ teaspoon salt
½ teaspoon lemon pepper
2 teaspoons olive oil
boiled water

Put all of the dry ingredients into the container carefully, being sure not to sneeze or get it into your eyes. Add the oil. Then slowly add a few drops of water and stir. Continue to add water while stirring into a smooth paste.

The result will be one cup of very, very, hot martza. A tiny touch will flavor a large plate of food.

FRESH MINT SAUCE
Raita

SERVES 2 TO 4

This hot and cold condiment is excellent with chicken curry. It also does well on its own with roti and raw vegetables for the vegetarian.

INGREDIENTS:

> 1 32-ounce container plain yogurt
> 1 teaspoon hot chili paste
> 1 cup ground fresh mint leaves

You can make your own yogurt (see p. 67) or buy any good quality plain yogurt. Plain red chili paste is found at most Asian groceries. We use sambal olek from Vietnam. It's great. We happen to have a huge patch of mint in our garden, making this condiment a joy to prepare.

Grind the mint leaves a few at a time with a mortar and pestle. This releases all the oils of the mint, preserving its flavor and nutritional value.

Simply combine the mint and chili with the yogurt. The quantity of mint you use affects the strength and coolness of the raita. If you are not going to use it all at one sitting, set out a small amount in a serving bowl and refrigerate the rest immediately in a closed container.

YOGURT

Sho

Yogurt is often served after a meal. It is commonly unsweetened, but a sweetener such as sugar or honey is served and added to taste.

If you have a large family that is fond of yogurt, you will find it economical to make your own. If it is possible to obtain fresh milk from a nearby farm the results will be especially rewarding. Organic whole milk available in health food stores is also recommended. However, this technique works with any whole milk that is available.

The quality of the yogurt that is used as a starter will also effect the outcome of your homemade batch. Select a brand with the texture and quality you most enjoy.

INGREDIENTS:

> I gallon whole milk
> ½ small carton plain yogurt

Pour the milk into a large pot and bring just to the point of boiling over low heat. Turn off the heat, and allow the milk to cool. It takes about 45 minutes for the milk to cool sufficiently. The milk must be warmer than body temperature but not hot enough to burn your finger as you test the temperature.

Take out 2 cups of the scalded milk and stir the half container of yogurt into it. (Even 1 tablespoon is enough yogurt to use as a starter.) Blend the yogurt and milk together well, and then stir the mixture into the pot of milk. Stir well to assure that the yogurt mixture is incorporated evenly into the milk.

Cover the pot with its lid, and wrap the entire pot in a thick towel. This will help the mixture stay warm. Leave the pot on the stove over night.

In the morning you will have a big pot of yogurt. If the yogurt is a little loose, it will firm up after refrigeration.

TIBETAN CHEESE
Chura

This is a very simple recipe for a dried cheese that can be added to many dishes for extra flavor and protein. It takes about 2 hours and requires attention, but is worth the effort. If one is taking the time to make chura it makes sense to use a gallon of milk.

You will need 2 pans (deep cast iron frying pans work best), a wooden spatula, a large wooden cutting board and some cheesecloth tents. Chura can be made on a stove top or on an open fire.

INGREDIENTS:

1 gallon whole milk
1 cup yogurt or buttermilk

Pour the milk into a large bowl and add the yogurt or buttermilk, stirring to incorporate throughout.

Pour the mixture into the pans so they are almost full and turn the heat on high. The mixture will begin to boil, and the curds and whey will separate. Continue to boil the milk, stirring occasionally so that the curds on the bottom are not burnt. The liquid boils away and the small curds slowly become golden yellow in color.

When you have only moist curd left in the frying pan, turn off the heat. Place the curds on a wooden board in an even layer.

Cover with the tents and place in direct sunlight, either outdoors or in a sunny window. Allow to dry, which will take many hours, depending on the sunlight. The cheese may be turned with a spatula when it appears dry on top to move things along and ensure even curing.

When the cheese is completely dry, scrape it off the board and store in a glass jar. It will keep for months. The cheese is sweet and pleasant tasting and goes very well with tsampa and in soups.

INDIAN CHAI
Chai Garam

Amazing! Chai has become mainstream! Now available at Starbucks everywhere… Chai, (the Indian word for tea) is a beverage familiar to Tibetans through their connections with India and Nepal. Generally served in the afternoon at tea time, this hot, spiced, sweetened tea can be made at home in a variety of ways. It can be served after lunch in place of dessert, or with biscuits.

Whole milk, skim milk, evaporated milk, 2% milk, even rice milk or soy milk, can be used. Traditionally sugar is the sweetener, but honey, maple syrup, stevia or agave nectar can be substituted with fine subtleties of flavor as the result.

Black tea is used in making chai, and the type you select will profoundly affect the flavor. Loose Darjeeling tea is excellent. Chinese black tea with jasmine or lychee enhance the bouquet. Avoid strongly flavored teas such as Lapsang Souchong and Earl Grey.

Using whole spices will give the chai the most potent flavor. A good combination is 1 pod cardamom, 2 whole black peppercorns, ¼ inch stick of cinnamon, and ¼ inch piece of fresh ginger per person. These spices should be pounded slightly in a mortar. If your cupboard does not have whole spices, powdered spices can be used. Use ¼ teaspoon per person each of cinnamon, ginger, and cardamom. Crushed whole black pepper corn, bay leaf, allspice, and nutmeg are also sometimes used. Too much allspice and nutmeg will make your chai taste like pumpkin pie!

Use milk and water in equal parts, 2/3 cup of each per person. Put the water and milk into a stainless steel pot, large enough for the quantity you are making. Add the spices to the milk and water mixture, and heat over medium to low heat. It is important to stir and watch the pot, as boiling milk can easily rush over the top of the pot in an instant.

When the milk mixture and spices have come to a boil, add the tea. If using loose tea, about ¾ teaspoon per person is fine, or 1 tea bag. Turn down the heat and simmer for about 5 minutes. Add 1 teaspoon per person of the chosen sweetener, stir and turn off the heat. Pour the chai through a strainer into a heated tea pot and serve.

Traditional and Ceremonial Foods and Customs

ROASTED BARLEY FLOUR
Tsampa

Tibetans speak of tsampa with reverence and pride. It is an indigenous food that is at once very simple yet has seemingly endless variations both in preparation and health-giving applications. Tsampa is roasted barley flour. It looks like very fine whole grain flour, but the significant difference is that it is roasted before grinding, and the grain is therefore already cooked. It is a food that is strong and adaptable, much like the character of the Tibetan people themselves.

Tsampa is made from barley, a grain that grows well in the high altitude of the southernmost plains on the Tibetan plateau. Because the land is difficult to work, there are many small plots linked together. The fields are irrigated by narrow stone channels that move the runoff from the mountain glaciers and streams through the fields. This flow is adjusted by hand . When the channel is blocked with a stone or opened, gravity naturally redirects the irrigation pathways.

The families living in the farming community decide on the order of water usage, which rotates among the families each year. In this way the resources are used fairly. This also provides for a slight variation in the time of harvest. Although customs vary from region to region, a barley planting ritual in early spring to ask for the blessing of good growing conditions is universal. Ceremonies and festivals also take place at harvest time. All the work is done communally.

The barley is threshed and stored in large sacks. After the supply for the year has been set aside, a portion of the harvest is used for trade and another portion offered to the local monastery. Tsampa embodies an ageless cycle of sustenance from the skillful interaction of people and animals with nature.

The method described here is for making 25 pounds of tsampa. It takes all day and is not worth the effort to make a smaller amount. Order a bag of organic hulled barley from your local health food store so it will be fresh. When making tsampa for the first time it is a good idea to have someone with experience to show you how it is done. I am very lucky that our Ama Dronlha taught me this skill, as I am very fond of tsampa!

INGREDIENTS:

    25 pounds of organic hulled barley
    salt

EQUIPMENT:

    4 very large metal bowls
    1 large metal mesh colander
    plastic or metal cup
    pot holders
    12-inch or 18-inch heavy duty wok
    10 cups of sand
    wood fire
    electric flour mill

PREPARING THE BARLEY

There are two methods for this. The easiest is to use a garden hose. Bring the bag of barley outdoors. Open it carefully at the top and throw in a little salt. Soak the grain thoroughly so the water seeps out of the bag. Mix the barley with your hand, making sure it is all wet. Then let the water drain out, encouraged by placing a heavy stone on top of the bag. It is important for the water to drain out.

The second method is to wash the barley in warm water. Use the large metal bowls for this. Pour as much barley as you can fit into the bowl and rinse under the tap in the sink, tilting the bowl to drain off the water. I have two bowls that are about 24 inches in diameter and about half a bag fits into each one, so this is fairly easy to do. I usually bring the bowls of drained barley out to a sunny place beside the fire and tip them at an angle on a stone. This way the barley at the top will be dry, and you can work your way down when roasting.

SETTING UP THE FIRE

While the soaked barley is draining, prepare the fire. Find a flat place, open overhead where it is safe to have a small fire. You will need 3 large rocks, set apart from each other in a triangle, so that the wok can sit on top of it. Between the stones, logs or branches are fed into the center to keep the fire burning hot for the hours it takes to roast the tsampa. Be sure to have your firewood nearby so you can maintain a hot flame. The placement of the rocks allows for a good draft in the center, as the heat should be concentrated.

When the fire is going well, place the wok on top and put 4 to 6 cups of sand in it. The barley is roasted in the hot sand. Initially it takes about 15 to 20 minutes for the sand to reach the right temperature. Test the temperature by tossing a few droplets of water on the sand. If they bounce and quickly evaporate, the sand is hot enough.

ROASTING THE BARLEY

This part of the process must be done quickly and requires upper body strength and agility. There are a number of things to do in succession as if in one motion. To begin, scoop a cup of the drained barley from the bowl and place it on the hot sand. Set the cup aside and grab two pot holders. Take hold of the wok and toss the sand and barley together, as though you are making an omelet. Do this continuously as the barley pops to keep it from burning.

In about 2 minutes, when it appears that all the barley has popped, the kernels will be white. Quickly pour the entire mixture of sand and barley into the sieve, which is set inside a bowl. The bowl catches the sand and the popped barley remains in the sieve.

Put the sieved barley aside in a large bowl. Place the wok back on the fire immediately and return the hot sand to it. Now it is time to rest and wait for the sand to reheat before repeating the process.

All of this should be done in a series of swift movements that will be repeated until all the barley is roasted. This is not easy, but can be learned with persistence.

CLEANING THE ROASTED BARLEY

Your two bowls of soaked and drained barley have become two bowls of fragrant, light, popped barley. Allow the barley to cool to the touch so it is not steaming.

Put the barley inside a large cotton bag, about the size of a pillow case. Two cotton pillow cases inside each other works fine. Tie the open end very tightly.

Now it is time to pound the barley. You can encourage young children to trample the bag or you can pound it with wood. Some might find this very satisfying work! The barley should be beat for at least 30 minutes. Everyone can take turns.

Open the bag and using your colander take out some barley. Sift and shake it and the wind will carry away everything that does not belong in the tsampa. Place the sifted barley back into the clean bowl.

GRINDING THE BARLEY

This is the easiest part of the process, but it too should be done outdoors. The grinding machine is very, very loud and also creates quantities of fine dust. Plug in the machine and begin grinding the barley on the finest setting. This is it, tsampa! When all the barely is ground you will have 25 pounds of tsampa.

Let it cool down completely to room temperature before storing. You can put it into rice bags or large containers with tightly fitting lids to store. Don't forget to clean the grinding machine with a dry cloth and store it with the other things you have assembled to make tsampa. (You will not need to spend time rounding them all up again the next time.)

USING TSAMPA

At home we keep a canister on the counter alongside the flour and sugar, filled with tsampa for the table. While producing tsampa is time-consuming, all the ways to use tsampa are very fast and require little or no cooking! Tsampa also travels well and can be carried in a zip-lock bag.

Tsampa is said to have medicinal properties. It staves off hunger and gives energy. Tsampa is the staple of the Tibetan monastic diet, along with butter tea. The tea is prepared in a huge barrel, and served from many large kettles. Each monk has his own cup and bowl, and mixes the tsampa and tea by hand. There are many ways to do this.

One method is to place a few spoonfuls in the bottom of your cup, add a little tea and stir the tsampa into a paste. Add more tea and continue to stir. The result is a very thick tea which is quite filling.

Another favorite is to put about ½ cup of tea and one teaspoon of butter in a small bowl, add about ¾ cups of tsampa, and knead it into the tea and butter with the right hand while turning the bowl with the left. The result is warm, moist tsampa of dough-like consistency. Dried yak cheese is commonly incorporated into the mix. This can be enjoyed accompanied by tea, or dipping into chili, yogurt, or warm chang.

When a woman is going into labor, tsampa soup is made. The tsampa is incorporated into a broth made fresh by boiling finely chopped meat in salted water. This is kept on hand, and is administered by the spoonful during labor to help keep up strength. A thicker version is given after the birth to help bring in the mothers milk.

Tsampa soup without meat is also very good for persons with digestive problems, tiredness, or recovering from illness or minor surgery. This soup is made by briskly stirring 3 tablespoons of tsampa into 2 cups of cold water. The tsampa blends smoothly into the water. Turn on the heat and bring the soup to a boil for a minute while continuing to stir. Salt to taste, or add a little butter or milk for a richer soup.

Tsampa is the main ingredient for making traditional tsok and torma.

FOOD for OFFERINGS
Tsok

Tsok is a term that refers in a broad sense to blessed, offered food. There are numerous occasions requiring a tsok puja. (Puja is the name for a Tibetan Buddhist ritual service, comparable to a Christian mass.) On Losar, the Tibetan New Year, tsok is offered by everyone attending the puja. The food is blessed by the lamas during the course of the prayers and distributed to everyone present at the end of the ceremony. This blessed food is considered sacred and eating it is a culmination of the blessings received.

These days, the tsok offered at a puja may consist of candies, potato chips, crackers, cookies, popcorn, fruits—anything that is enjoyed, easily acquired, and easily distributed. This food is arranged in bowls at the foot of the shrine before the puja begins. Drinks, such as tea, juice, and sodas, may also be offered.

Traditionally, tsok consists of the ceremonial offering cakes called torma (see p. 78). These are made from tsampa, butter, sugar, and cheese, formed into simple shapes and colored red.

Tsok is also a term used for consecrated food that is to be burnt. There are many types of pujas where burnt offerings are required. Pujas may be performed to bring good health and prosperity and to remove obstacles. The lama who is performing the ceremony knows exactly what is needed in each instance, according to the traditional text.

CEREMONIAL OFFERING CAKES
Torma

There are many forms of torma. Although they are primarily made of edible materials, they are not all meant to be eaten. They range from very simple forms to wondrously beautiful sculptured images. The making of torma is one the Tibetan sacred art forms that I especially admire.

Traditionally, torma are made by monks who are taught by lamas with a talent for the making of torma. One's state of mind and intent are important elements to be considered during the process, as well as understanding the stated purpose of the torma being made. These skills are generally taught to monks and retreatants. Lay people may also request to learn how to make torma for offering on shrines at home, in accordance with personal practice. Simple torma to be offered for a morning Tara puja may be made from rolled oats and pure water, dotted with butter.

In Tibet, torma were made out of butter colored with vegetable dyes. These sculptures were sometimes eight feet tall or more, mounted on wood. They would take many monks many weeks to complete and were used on special religious festival days. People would gather from near and far to watch the Lama Dances and religious plays. The torma would be brought outside for the populace to view, and invariably end in the offering fire: a labor of love and a testament to impermanence, for the benefit of all beings.

The traditional tsok offering is a kind of torma made from tsampa, butter, brown sugar, and tiny bits of dried yak cheese. The primary ingredient is butter. It is softened, and the tsampa is kneaded into the butter by hand until it is somewhat dry but holds a shape. The brown sugar may be brought into the mix at the beginning when softening the butter, or toward the end, depending on the kind of sugar you are using. Soft brown sugar commonly found in American stores is easily blended in. Another form of sugar found in some Asian groceries is more golden in color and comes in sticks about 6 inches long and ¼ inch thick. This sugar is crumbled and added at the end with the granulated cheese, both of which give interest and texture to the torma. This is an extremely rich food, and should be taken in small quantities.

Torma butter sculpture offerings in Bodh Gaya.

When prepared in reasonable quantities to place on a shrine for blessing, these torma are formed by hand into egg shapes, about the size of an ostrich egg, but flat on the bottom so they stand upright. The torma are painted with red food coloring. In large monasteries where hundreds are in attendance to receive blessings, the torma is made into bricks using wooden molds. These are then turned out, painted red, and sliced to serve many people. This method of preparing torma is still being done today in the monasteries in Tibet and Nepal.

The torma is a perfect metaphor for the interconnectedness of life.

TIBETAN TEA
Po Cha

Tibetan tea always produces a dramatic reaction on its first introduction. Most Westerners think of tea with lemon, or cream and sugar, and now herbal teas have also become the norm. Mentioning tea with salt and butter will often result in a refusal to even try it. It is more fun to offer Tibetan tea first and explain later.

The tea itself is grown in the southern region near the Burmese border where rice is also grown. It is tended and harvested by hand, then air-dried and pressed into blocks containing whole leaves and some twigs. This tea makes its way into all regions of Tibet through trade. Friends and relatives bring tea as household gifts.

The tea is placed into cold water and brought to a boil. It is then strained and churned with salted yak butter and milk until frothy. Goat or sheep's milk might also be used. Traditionally, tea is churned in a very tall wooden churn called a chathu. It is used only for making tea and is rarely washed, which gives the tea a rancid taste.

Today it is possible to obtain a plastic chathu from Tibet House. It holds ten cups. If you have no relatives to bring tea to your home, you can purchase black pressed tea at Chinese food stores which has a very similar, smoky taste. Salted butter and half-and-half work very well to approximate the real thing.

Tibetan tea, especially with the addition of tsampa, is an extremely fortifying beverage. The addition of the fat and salt into the diet is suitable for the cold and arid climate.

The offering of tea to guests has various social ramifications. Tea must be offered to a guest immediately after the welcome greeting. Often some biscuits are offered as well. Depending upon local tradition, the number of cups of tea drunk may mark how closely a guest is connected with the family being visited. Tea is also offered daily to the deities on the household shrine. In particular, the Dharma protectors receive their tea in a specially designed cup with a bowl beneath it, which allows the cup to be filled to overflowing. This offering tea is served black.

CUSTOMS and ETIQUETTE

Here in the melting pot of America, most of us can trace our roots back a generation or two to the time when two or more different cultures were joined, creating a family of American children. We hope that our mixed cultures and races will keep the best of all traditions alive. Indeed we all have more in common than we have differences.

Among the tribal and ethnic groups of Tibet, separated by vast expanses of land, great variation in climate, and no modern means of communication, there are many customs that vary considerably. My purpose is to share what I have learned through experience over the years, so that anyone reading this book will feel more open to developing genuine friendship with Tibetan people.

At one time in Tibet, a greeting between equals consisted of bumping the crowns of each other's foreheads together. Happiness and greeting were expressed by displaying the tongue while smiling! It is not likely that any Tibetan you meet in America today will greet you in this way. A handshake will be expected and welcomed. A slight bow goes along with that, and is appropriate especially if meeting people in robes. Hugging is not the way to go.

You may have to ask for a Tibetan's personal or given name in an introduction, as they may not consider this an important detail. Many Tibetans identify each other by relationship: sister, brother, same father-mother, cousin, second cousin, aunt, uncle, or second-cousin-brother-of-youngest-aunt's-grandfather. This makes sense, considering that tribes consisted of the merging of large families, often of ten or twelve children.

The lack of importance of the name is also a reflection on the associated strength derived from identifying with being a Tibetan.

Tibetans are also sometimes reluctant to talk about themselves, not wanting to appear egotistical. Sometimes they feel uncomfortable speaking English. You can set an example by being forthcoming, and try exchanging stories about travel. Humor, joking, and teasing are also very much a part of Tibetan culture, and a good way to engage in relaxed dialogue. Card games play a big part in Tibetan informal gatherings, and are a good way for people to spend time together, especially if they are not well acquainted.

Most Tibetans take their shoes off before entering the home. Some Westerners have adopted this custom too and it is common in Asian cultures. If you visit a Tibetan home, then, remove your shoes. You will probably be reminded by all the shoes outside the door!

Good hospitality is considered a gesture of respect by Tibetan people. Offering a beverage and a snack to a guest is very important. If you enter a Tibetan home you will be presented with tea and food, or if the person is used to Westerners they may offer you a choice of water or juice or coffee. If a Tibetan is a guest at your home, or just stopping by for business, it is polite to offer something. The fine points of how insistent to be in this offering will be up to you to judge. It is customary for some people to decline at first and give the host an opportunity to insist, and in other regions, one is expected to speak directly and accept what is being offered immediately. What is most important is to welcome the person and express happiness at seeing them. No matter what, if it comes from the heart everything will be fine.

Most Tibetans now know as well as most of us, and perhaps better than some of us, how to use cutlery and which side of the plate to place them on. However, eating with the hands and drinking from a bowl is also perfectly fine. Dishes with Indian influence, such as dal, breads, and curries, are eaten by hand, as are momos. Licking the plate is also a good thing!

Generally Tibetans are used to sitting on the floor or low cushions, and can do so very comfortably. Picnics are a Tibetan tradition. The way food is served depends on the number of people, the amount of space, and the nature of the occasion. Serving buffet style is an acceptable way to go with a small crowd of eight or twelve people, and is becoming the new custom internationally.

Tibetans are comfortable with informal gatherings. However, if you are a Buddhist and often invite Tibetan lamas to your home, it is a sign of respect to offer the best that you can manage. See Serving Lamas, below, for some guidelines.

Cleanliness in food preparation and serving is important. Tasting should not be done with the serving spoon. We naturally want to share healthy, beautiful food within our means. This is Tibetan tradition also.

SERVING LAMAS

In Tibetan tradition, there are many circumstances that require the presence of a lama: birth, naming a child, death, marriage, illness, special days determined by one's personal astrology, special days in the calendar year, and days to make offerings to bring benefit and protect the family. The lama's visit comes in response to a request for a specific puja, which includes the invitation of an entourage of monks suitable to both the situation and the family's means. Bringing the lama in this way is an example of the complete integration of faith and practice into daily life. While the occasion of a lama's visit stirs up activities of preparation and excitement, it is simultaneously felt to be a normal and proper way to move in the circle of life, bringing benefit to oneself and others.

Here in the West it is also possible to invite a lama to one's home, but we do not have the good fortune of familiarity with, or childhood memories of, the lifestyle from which the lamas have come, so we must discover how to do this through our own experience. For many, the wish to bring the lamas into our personal world may not arise.

Western Buddhists may be inclined to invite a lama to officiate at an opening ceremony for a business or study center, a wedding, or any auspicious occasion. Lamas are willing and able to participate in these functions. We might also be inclined to invite a lama to our home for lunch or tea to deepen our personal connection with the teacher and cultivate a spiritual friendship, or as a gesture of respect, engendering a closer student-teacher relationship.

When hosting a lama, the main point to consider is that, ultimately, the lama himself has no requirements that need be met. But if one has offered an invitation, it is logical to follow through with appropriate action. To begin, where will your guest be seated? Look at your space and decide where the best seat is. This may simply be the most comfortable seat. You may decide to improve on it by draping a new or beautiful piece of cloth over the seat. If your lama is visiting for the first time, having a spot ready that can be easily recognized on entering makes it easy for everyone to get comfortable.

If you are inviting a number of lamas and monks it is a good idea to understand their interrelationship. In formal settings there is an established order of seating and serving that acknowledges the rank and accomplishment of those present. This is important particularly if you have invited lamas to a public affair of some kind. As the host, you would be expected to know this. If you don't, ask ahead and find out. If you forget, just be sure to have enough seats and the group will find their own order without a mention. In a home setting, the lama of the highest rank should be seated to the left of the attendants and served first. If this seems to be too much for you, don't worry. Offer one special seat and everything will fall into place. An old monk friend once told me, as general advice, "See the situation."

It is a good idea to ask the lama's personal attendant about any dietary considerations before planning a meal. This is something commonly done these days in our nutrition-conscious society. If you do not inquire, whatever you serve will be accepted graciously, even if it goes against doctors' recommendations. When preparing food, it is important to keep everything as pure as possible. Hands and food and utensils should be washed before preparation. Usually a prayer is said before the meal so be aware that this will happen, and then enjoy your blessed food.

In households where lamas often visit, a separate set of dishes is set aside for this purpose. In some instances these few pieces are bought new with this function in mind, and used only by visiting lamas. You may wish to use some treasured antique dishes or especially beautiful heirlooms. The idea is to express one's inner respect by offering the best materially, according to one's means and taste.

If you invite a lama to stay at a Dharma center, you should try to offer a private space with a clean place to sleep. When making the bed, the linens should not be placed on the floor. Move around the bed while making it, keeping the linens fresh. It is not necessary to buy new linens, but anything used should be freshly cleaned.

In the event that you are hosting a puja, it is best to ask ahead what you should have on hand. The lama's attendant will know or can find out for you. Generally speaking, lamas are very happy to direct if you express a willingness to learn.

A lama is not looking to evaluate a student on his or her performance in these situations. He himself does not require or expect special attention or service. The lama's concern remains constant, to benefit beings, and the flow of blessings is not affected by the level of service that is provided. Visiting your home is for him a welcomed opportunity to generate bodhicitta. The benefit of doing one's best to serve a visiting lama all tallies up on the side of the one offering the invitation. This may be seen as a practical enactment of evoking the deity through visualization. The purity of intention and effort all reflect on the karmic mirror of the student.

The reflection of your karmic accumulations need not make you nervous if your intentions are purely motivated. It is best to relax and be yourself, and let your happiness be at the fore. An open heart is the best invitation.

CREATING A SHRINE

The idea of creating a sacred space within one's home is not a foreign concept in today's busy Western reality, but a tradition lost. The importance of devotion and the connection with the spirit has been ignored or compartmentalized in the pursuit of progress. There are many benefits of connecting with the divine, and having a visual reminder at home helps us do this.

Whether you are a practicing Buddhist or just like Buddhas, here are some suggestions that may be of benefit. If you have a spare room to set aside for meditation or yoga you are very lucky, and can devote a larger space to creating a shrine. However, a small shelf on the wall or the top of a dresser will work fine.

The shelf must be placed high, but not too high to reach and not at your feet. So if you choose your bedroom because it is the quietest room, place the offering shelf or shrine near your head, not where your feet are while you sleep. Your shelf can be very simple. There are nice, wooden, ready-made shelves at most arts and crafts stores that are inexpensive and easy to put up. A single statue or photo and a small vase or incense burner is enough. The main purpose is not for ornamentation, but to cultivate bodhichitta, compassion and generosity for the benefit of all beings. Having a place to offer a flower with right intention is of great benefit to oneself and others.

Tibetan Buddhist shrines have a number of objects that all have meaning within the various traditions. Thangkas—scroll paintings picturing the Buddha or other deities—are important, as are statues. As well as being very beautiful to look at, a thangka changes the energy in a room. Used traditionally as a meditation tool, one can sit and focus attention on the deity and the details in the painting and visualize cultivating these qualities.

Statues are meant for cultivating devotion, and are used on a shrine where offerings are placed. It is best if the statue is blessed. There are ceremonies performed by lamas for this purpose. The statues which are empty are filled with precious substances and sealed. Once blessed, a statue should never be sold, but should remain in the hands of someone who will treat it with proper respect. A consecrated statue can be perceived as an embodiment of the deity it personifies, and we can then strengthen our aspirations. A statue or thangka painting of the Buddha or a deity should be placed in a high central position as the receiver of the offerings made at the shrine.

A shrine also includes a set of seven offering bowls, called dunsar, and a butter lamp. These are arranged in a straight line, with the butter lamp in fifth place from the right. They represent, in order from left to right: drinking water, water for feet, flowers, incense, light, perfume, food, and music. The bowls may all be filled with fresh water as symbolic offerings, or with appropriate objects. For example, you could fill the first three bowls with water, placing a flower in the third. The fourth bowl might hold rice in which you can stand some unlit sticks of incense. In the fifth bowl, you could place a few drops of perfume in water or set a small bottle of perfume in the bowl. In the next position, the butter lamp should be filled with oil and a wick, or you could use a simple tea light. The sixth bowl might hold dried fruits, an apple, some rice, or at the New Year, khapsey cookies. Music could be represented by placing a pair of ting sha cymbals, a bell, or a damaru in the seventh bowl.

The offering bowls are typically made of copper, brass, or silver. One should offer the best one can afford. These bowls are made by hand by artisans whose families have been doing this work for generations. Often they are decorated with the eight symbols of auspicious coincidence. In a Tibetan Buddhist family, these shrine objects are considered very precious and they are viewed as family treasures.

A shrine may also include a mandala plate, which is symbolic of the universe and is used in ceremonies for mandala offerings and in foundation practices. It consists of a bottom plate, usually about 6 inches in diameter, with three consecutively smaller rings that are stacked on top of each lower section as it is filled. Each section is filled with rice, or with very small stones the size of grain, along with pieces of precious and semi-precious stones, metals, coins, and the like, to create a symbolic offering of the universe to the divine. It is topped off with a small sculpture of the wish-fulfilling jewels. Other items include a special cup for offering tea to the Dharma protectors and other specially designed vessels used in rituals.

Traditional shrines are often decorated with bright silk brocade altar cloths, and are designed in three tiers. The statues are placed at the top and the offering bowls on the lower shelves. It is a good idea to have a pitcher set aside for the sole purpose of offering the shrine water. This arrangement makes it easy to make daily offerings, and assures the water will be pure.

Many people may not have the time for opening a shrine every day. That is why hanging a thangka painting and a simple shelf is often more desirable. By cultivating the habit of offering we are reminded of our own Buddha nature.

A shrine blends with some Western customs. On the numerous occasions that we celebrate with cake, such as birthdays, anniversaries, or graduations, the person of honor may place the first small piece on the shrine, perhaps saying a prayer or making a wish. And it is not uncommon to find a Western cake in a Tibetan monastery on the birthday of a beloved teacher.

When entering a shrine room, or a temple or monastery, remove your shoes. Modest dress is considered appropriate, and 'modest' is defined by conservative standards. Women and men alike should not wear shorts or bathing suits, revealing shirts, or short skirts. A shrine room, created for prayer and meditation, is a sacred space and worthy of respect.

One should be mindful of any activity taking place and not engage in unnecessary speech. Tibetan Buddhists perform three prostrations upon entering a shrine and often offer khatas, or thin, white, silk scarves, to the altar and lamas. This is a gesture of respect and gratitude. If participating in a ritual or empowerment for the first time, simply observe those around you and emulate their conduct. Most important is having the appropriate attitude.

Tibetan New Year
Losar

LOSAR TRADITIONS

Tibetan New Year, called Losar, is celebrated every year in February, coinciding with the New Moon. The date is calculated by the Tibetan lunar calendar and is the first day of the first month of the year and does not occur on exactly the same date every year. It is good timing here in the northeast of North America. February is the last winter month and somehow spring is always in the air after Losar.

This is definitely the biggest holiday in Tibetan culture. Losar can be traced back to pre-Buddhist Tibetan ceremonies that celebrated the arts of cultivating, irrigation, and bridge building. Many customs and traditions are followed, both at the monasteries and in people's homes. Losar was formerly celebrated for fifteen days but now the festivities range between three and seven days depending on the country.

In monasteries, protector pujas are begun on the 29th day of the twelfth month in preparation for Losar ceremonies. Depending on where you live you might be able to attend a fire purification puja and have the opportunity to cast out your negativity from the old year. On that day, gu tuk, the traditional soup with nine surprise ingredients, is served by the household elder. Made of mashed and boiled grains, and flavored with dried yak cheese, the soup contains dumplings with messages or small objects. It is a kind of divination soup, where everyone has fun sharing their message, as people all over the globe now do with fortune cookies.

The last day of the year everything is cleaned. People clean their homes or apartments especially well, dusting on top of high furniture and under cabinets, and prepare their dress clothes for the coming occasion. Most Tibetans in exile wear traditional dress on Losar. In monasteries, elaborate shrine room decorations are made with special ceremonial cakes called torma and huge offerings of food, all artistically arranged and consecrated in the early morning puja. These are given to all the people who attend the ceremonies.

In times past, preparations for this day would include the yearly bath in the river for nomads living in the harsh climate of the Tibetan plateau. When Losar was celebrated over a fifteen-day period, one day was set aside for men to bathe, groom, and socialize, and another day for women. The best animals were also cleaned and adorned with colorful woven tack, bells, and jewelry. All children born during the previous year celebrated their birthday on Losar.

Losar begins at sunrise with prayer. Everyone assembles in the shrine room where the first cup of tea and a taste of sweet rice and chang are offered to the Three Jewels. Other ceremonial foods offered at the shrine might include yogurt, dhoma, and the decorative cookies called khapsey, which are all then shared at a sunrise meal. The sweetness of the chang, the fine texture of the yogurt, and the rich flavor of the tea all herald the auspicious nature of the New Year. Many wishes of "Tashi deleg"—"Good luck!"—are exchanged.

The day is spent close to home, resting and appreciating the day. Foods that can be eaten by hand along with the dishes made especially for Losar morning are available. These would be dried or boiled meat, fresh and dried fruit and nuts.

At large monasteries, traditional Lama Dances are performed on Losar. These are extraordinary to behold. Monks of all ages are involved in the all-day event, which is the culmination of many months of practice to learn the precise steps and forms of these ancient symbolic dances. The costumes are all made at the monasteries according to tradition and are very elaborate and beautiful. In times past, Tibetans from the countryside would travel many miles to attend these dances, which celebrate the triumph of good over evil and depict Tibetan secular and religious history. These were very important teachings for a largely illiterate population. Fortunately, this powerful tradition is still intact and can be seen at Buddhist monasteries in Nepal, India, and Tibet.

The remainder of Losar is spent visiting family and friends. Everyone brings khapsey and other foods as gifts. The welcoming host greets guests at the door with che mar, an offering of flour to toss in the air before entering. Tea, sweet rice, and chang are served, news and stories of "the old days" exchanged, and card games are often played. In the countryside where tribes would congregate, games like tug-of-war, running races, heavy lifting contests, and horsemanship competitions took place. These huge gatherings of hundreds of people are still taking place in some regions in the summer when the weather is good.

Some new Losar traditions have been adopted among Tibetans in exile. Tibetan families like to stay in touch with their distant relatives at Losar and cannot always take the time to travel, so a new industry of Losar greeting cards has sprung up. Also, some shrine decorations that were formerly sculpted from butter and grains, such as the sheep's head, which is an ancient symbol for abundance, can now be purchased in painted ceramic and saved from year to year, the way some of us save Christmas ornaments.

Setting up the Family Altar for Losar

Many modern Tibetans are now keeping pace with Western work schedules and, as lay people, do not have time for the formal practice of opening and closing a shrine every day. However, everyone makes the effort to have a beautiful Losar altar, preserving the spirit of this precious tradition.

In addition to the items normally included in a shrine—offering bowls, a statue or thangka painting of the Buddha or deity, and a mandala plate—certain items appear only for Losar:

- Sprouted wheat grass. One tablespoon of wheat berries, planted on top of potting soil in a small clay pot ten days before Losar, will give you a fine stand of green grass.

- Sheep's head sculpture. These are still made by hand from rolled oats and butter. The head of the ram is adorned with a moon disk, sun, lotus, and flames.

- Tea. This is usually a brick of Tibetan tea, wrapped in a khata scarf. A bowl of dried, loose tea would be fine.

- Khapsey. These fried cookies are made well in advance of Losar, but are set up on the shrine the day before. A footed cake plate is perfect to arrange a tower of khapsey, embellished with foil-wrapped candies, nuts, and dried fruit.

Reserve a space on the shrine or bring in a coffee table on which to place a small offering of each of the New Year foods on Losar morning. Losar is a happy occasion that everyone looks forward to. Celebrating a good Losar is the beginning of a good year.

OFFERING FLOUR
Che Mar

Traditionally made at Losar, the Tibetan New Year, this bowl of dried sweet grain is made for offering to the gods. A beautiful bowl of che mar, decorated with butter, sits in every temple and family shrine. There are specially designed vessels used for offering che mar. They are made of wood carved with auspicious symbols and hand-painted.

Che mar is used at the end of a traditional service, which consists of reciting of "The 21 Praises of Tara," during which Tibetan tea and fried cookies called khapsey are served to and shared by the whole sangha, or community. After the sangha members come forward to offer khata scarves to the Buddha and the lamas, they are greeted by a bowl of che mar, held by a monk. One is meant to take a pinch, and cast it into the air as a blessing and offering, cleaning the remaining grains from the fingers with the tongue.

Che mar can consist of the flours of five grains: rice, wheat, rye, corn, and barley, sifted together with a little sugar and mounded into a bowl to form a peak. Some softened butter is dabbed on for added richness and decoration. Tsampa (see p. 72) can also be used alone. This is very often the case, as tsampa and barley are most important to Tibetans.

During Losar, friends and relatives go around to visit each other, exchanging plates of the fried cookies called khapsey. Traditionally, when a guest enters a home, the hostess holds aloft a bowl of che mar, presenting it to the guest who immediately offers a pinch to the heavens. This exchange is symbolic of sharing abundance.

TIBETAN FRIED COOKIES
Khapsey

Although khapsey can be made at any time, they are traditionally made at Losar, the Tibetan New Year. The making of khapsey is an all day event. Each family must prepare a quantity that reflects their means relative to the community. The khapsey are made into various shapes and sizes for use as offerings on the household shrine and for giving to friends and relatives. The khapsey are offered on the shrine in an artistic arrangement that includes the use of dried fruits, nuts, and candies to add color.

Khapsey are also made at the monasteries to offer to the public attending the Losar ceremonies. The extraordinary effort required to produce this massive number of cookies turns the event into a working celebration. The challenge of perfecting the traditional styles, and of inventing new ones, encourages khapsey makers.

The khapsey are usually made about a week before Losar. It is beneficial to have time to recover and tend to other details of the celebration with khapsey making behind you. The khapsey also taste much better after they have set for a few days.

Traditionally khapsey were made unsweetened. Only water, flour, and oil or butter were used in making the stiff dough. These days some families choose to add a little sugar. The khapsey are deep-fried until golden and crunchy, then stored in a cardboard box until it is time to decorate the shrine and arrange them on plates to give away.

MAKING THE DOUGH

Two people are needed to make the dough. One person holds the bowl and pours while the other person kneads. We usually do this on the floor. Considerable strength is needed for this part of the task. The smallest quantity of flour used would be a 5-pound bag. Here are the basic proportions for sweetened khapsey dough.

INGREDIENTS:

>   5 pounds unbleached white flour
>   ¾ cup sugar
>   2 cups warm water
>   1 cup vegetable oil or melted butter

Dissolve the sugar into the warm water. Add this mixture alternately to the flour with the vegetable oil or melted butter, mixing and kneading by hand into a smooth elastic dough that is quite firm. You will probably need to add a little more than 2 cups of water.

Put the dough into a plastic bag so that it will not become dry while small portions are being rolled out.

To roll out the dough you will need a large cutting board and a long rolling pin. (These do not need to be purchased at a gourmet food store. A 2-foot long piece of 1½-inch closet pole and a 3-foot square piece of half inch plywood from a hardware store is fine.) As with preparing the dough, we usually work on the floor because it takes a lot of pressure to roll this dough thin enough. Trays and paper bags are also needed to lay the finished cookies on before and after frying.

We usually make the large khapsey that will be used for the shrine-room offerings first. They are traditionally about 12 to 18 inches long, and formed into a simple twist. There is no set number that needs to be made. It depends on how you are planning to set them up. Twelve is enough for a small stack.

Traditionally a shape called punga amcho, or donkey ears, is made next. These are a little tricky. The dough is rolled out into an oval about ¼ inch thick in the middle and 1 foot long. The shape is then wrapped and pinched only in the center, with the long ends extending. It is then fried by draping it over a chopstick to form the two ears.

The two basic shapes for khapsey are twists and flowers. These can vary in size from 3 to 10 inches long. Smaller ones are considered superior because they take more time and skill to make. They are also easier to eat.

CUTTING AND SHAPING THE COOKIES

Keep the prepared dough covered with plastic bags or damp cloths so that it does not dry out. You will need large cutting boards or countertops to work on when rolling and cutting the dough.

Pull or cut off a section of dough, a little smaller than the size of a football. The dough will be somewhat oily, and will roll out without the use of additional flour, but it is dense and will take some force. Roll out a sheet that is about ¼ inch thick.

For simple twist shapes, score the dough with a sharp knife, creating a grid pattern of sections about 1½ inches wide and 5 or 6 inches long. In the center of each rectangular section, cut a slit about 2 inches long. Each of these sections makes one khapsey. Have an empty tray or lots of brown paper bags to place the twisted khapsey on as you make them. It is best to have many of them made before the frying begins.

Pick up one section in your left hand. With your right hand, take hold of the top edge, insert it through the center slit, and pull up. It will create a twist that looks impressive for such a simple movement. Place the twisted khapsey on a tray and continue until all your rectangles are done. You may vary the size of these to suit your purposes. For the purpose of giving khapsey as gifts, many smaller ones are good. Large ones are good for creating an offering on your Losar shrine.

The second common khapsey shape is a flower. Roll out the dough in the same manner as for twists. Cut the dough into strips about 4 inches wide. You will have perhaps 3 or 4 long strips. Pick up one strip and fold it lightly in half length wise, edge to edge. You will now have a long strip about 2 inches wide. With a sharp knife, begin at one end and cut into the folded edge, making 8 cuts, ¼ inch apart, that come within ½ inch of the cut edge. Make the next cut all the way across to form one piece. Repeat; you should get 5 or 6 'flower' sections out of one strip, depending on how long it was to begin with.

To shape each flower, lift one section and open it. Form a tube by squeezing the two edges together to seal them. Press this sealed edge into the cutting board surface with your finger inside of it. Now pinch each thin section in the center to form a point. Lift the points up, pulling them alternately to the right and left to form the flower. If you are good at braiding, you can experiment with any designs that come to mind to create other shapes. The flower is the simplest and looks very nice.

Place all your finished flowers on a tray. During this process all the finished khapsey will dry out a little, which helps them to hold their shape while frying.

ROLL OUT A SHEET OF DOUGH THAT IS ABOUT 1/4 INCH THICK

HOW TO MAKE SIMPLE TWISTED KHAPSEY

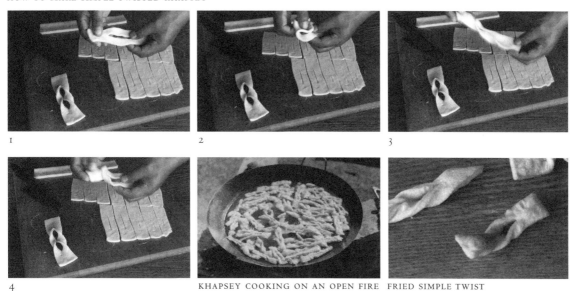

1

2

3

4

KHAPSEY COOKING ON AN OPEN FIRE

FRIED SIMPLE TWIST

HOW TO MAKE "FLOWER" SHAPED KHAPSEY

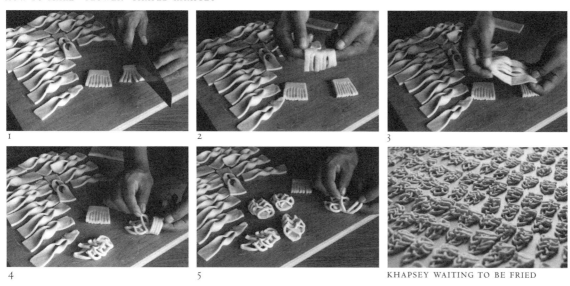

1

2

3

4

5

KHAPSEY WAITING TO BE FRIED

Tibetan Cooking   97

FRYING THE COOKIES

Deep fry the khapsey in any available vegetable oil. Corn oil and peanut oil are best as they leave no oily taste. The oil should be about four inches deep. Because some of the khapsey can be a foot long, we use a large roasting pan that spans two burners for frying. It is good to open some windows during the many hours of frying. Expect the house to smell like khapsey for a few days, unless you are able to do this outdoors. Ideally one would use a 2-foot wok on an outdoor fire.

Use long wooden chop sticks or metal tongs to turn and remove the khapsey from the oil. The person with the job of frying has to cultivate some expertise and exercise good concentration when working around so much hot oil and a number of moving helpers. When the oil is first heated, a small tortoise is sculpted from the khapsey dough and put into the oil. It is meant to absorb all the negativity left from the old year. When it is nearly black it is removed and set aside. At this point, the oil should be hot enough for frying. Test by placing one khapsey in the oil. If it bubbles and floats up immediately, the oil is hot enough.

Fry one design at a time, because the frying time will vary with the design. Put in as many as will cover one layer of the surface of your oil. Turn them for even frying. They cook fast, which is why it is important to have most of the preparation done first.

You will need a slotted spoon, tongs or long cooking chopsticks to remove the khapsey when they are golden. Place them on brown paper bags and let them cool. When cool, store them in cardboard boxes lined with brown paper.

LHASA KHAPSEY

One other kind of khapsey we make at the end of the process is called the Lhasa khapsey. The dough is made separately of the same ingredients —egg, flour, water, and oil—but with the consistency of pancake batter. The batter is placed in a recycled dish-soap bottle and squeezed into the hot oil. The result is a circle of many intertwined strands, later dusted with confectionery sugar. Lhasa khapsey and donkey ears are made commercially these days in bakeries in Kathmandu.

SPECIAL KHAPSEY

These deep fried cookies are light and crunchy. The many layers and oval shape make them very special indeed. Two people are needed because the timing must be just right.

INGREDIENTS:

> 4 cups unbleached white flour
> 2 tablespoons sugar
> 2 tablespoons oil
> 1 egg
> ¾ cup cold water
> ¼ cup unsalted butter

Beat the egg, oil, and sugar into the water. Blend this mixture by hand into the flour, forming a firm and cohesive dough.

Roll the out very thin so that it is nearly translucent. Use a board dusted with flour and a long rolling pin to achieve this.

Melt the butter. Using a pastry brush, spread the melted butter evenly over the surface of the dough. Dust lightly with a little flour. Roll the dough into a long tube, butter side in.

Using a sharp knife, cut the tube into 1½-inch sections. Roll each section flat, working inward toward the center. The center should be slightly thicker, forming an oval shape.

While the dough is being prepared, begin to heat the oil for frying. You will need a depth of at least 4 inches. Immediately fry each cookie, using a pair of wooden chopsticks or tongs to hold both ends of the cookie in the oil until it begins to cook. It takes only a few moments for the edges to brown and the cookie to puff up in the oil. Lift it out, draining off the excess oil, and place it on a paper towel to drain.

When all the cookies are done and cooled, you may dust them with confectionery sugar for some added sweetness and beauty. Store them in a tightly sealed container as they are very sensitive to humidity.

SWEET RICE
Deysi

SERVES 8

This is a food for special times. It is served on Losar morning, at weddings, and for returns from distant places. Raisins are commonly used in this dish. However, in eastern Tibet, dhoma (wild yams) traditionally take their place.

INGREDIENTS:

4 cups rice
1 cup golden raisins
½ cup butter
½ cup sugar
one pinch of saffron

Cook the rice with just enough water so that it retains its shape (slightly less than 2 cups of cold water for each cup of raw rice). Melt the butter and add the sugar, raisins, and saffron threads to the melted butter. When rice has cooled, pour this mixture into the rice and mix thoroughly. Sometimes a little yellow food coloring is added for effect.

Serve neatly rounded in small bowls, just warm or at room temperature.

TIBETAN WILD YAMS
Dhoma

These small tuberous vegetables are indigenous to Tibet and were formerly harvested only from the wild. They are dug from the earth and dried, in which form they last indefinitely. Dhoma is naturally sweet, and tastes very much like chestnut.

Dhoma is now grown in small quantities for commercial sale as a Chinese export. It sells in Nepal packaged as Tibetan Wild Sweet Potato, although this is a cultivated variety. It has sometimes reached us as a precious gift in a hand-sewn bag, complete with bits of Tibetan stone and earth: dhoma harvested by hand from the wild, an ancient culinary treasure.

Before cooking it is necessary to sort through the dhoma to remove any small stones. Wash the dhoma thoroughly. Then boil them gently for 15 to 20 minutes until tender. The dhoma may be eaten boiled like this, but are most often used in combination with other foods.

After the dhoma are cooked, you can add a generous quantity of butter, which combines with the liquid left from boiling the dhoma. You can mix tsampa into this buttery liquid. The taste and texture is very unique and earthy, and the tsampa is said to aid in the digestion of the fat.

Dhoma is also added sparingly to freshly made yogurt. This is traditionally served at Losar, the Tibetan New Year. Dhoma is also added to the sweet rice called deysi. In fact the raisins we normally use in deysi are the modern substitute when dhoma is not available.

RICE WINE
Chang

SERVES 8 TO 10

This type of chang is served in our household at breakfast on Losar morning, according to tradition. It is made four days in advance. If the chang is delicious, it foretells of a good year. We also prepare it regularly during the winter months, as it is served hot and is naturally sweet and soothing.

Chang taken early from the fermenting pot is not very strong, and is thick like rice soup. This is referred to as 'ladies' chang' and it still makes for a relaxing New Year's Day. However, the fermentation process can go on for many weeks or even several months, yielding a clear liquid under the soft mash of rice that is very potent, not unlike sake. A little of this chang is very effective.

It was once customary to make a batch of chang on the departure day of a loved one embarking on a long journey. This chang would be opened and drunk in celebration on the day of their return.

INGREDIENTS:

> 10 cups rice
> 18 cups water
> 2 balls of yeast (Ask for wine-making yeast at a Chinese grocery store:
>   white 1-inch diameter spheres.)
> 2 tablespoons tsampa (see p. 72)

Cook the rice in the water. Let it cool to room temperature or slightly warmer than body temperature by spreading it out onto a clean surface. This is not an exacting process; the rice should be about an inch deep.

Grind the yeast and tsampa together with a mortar and pestle until finely powdered. Sprinkle this over the warm rice. Then, using your washed hands, thoroughly mix the yeast into the rice so that it is evenly blended.

Put all of the rice into a large 12-quart stock pot with a lid. Secure the lid well, using a dish cloth or twine, so that no air can penetrate. Wrap the pot in a couple of blankets and store in a warm dark place (under the bed or in a closet) preferably near a heat source.

After 3 or 4 days you will notice a sweet chang smell and it will be ready.

Usually the chang is quite sweet on its own. Tibetans say the sweetness depends on the hand that makes it, and that chang should be made by only one person.

To serve, ladle about 1 cup per person into a pot, and warm on the stove. Do not boil, or it will ruin the taste and remove the alcohol. You may add a little unsalted butter or water to thin the consistency if you wish. If you have never seen chang before you may be surprised. It looks a bit like oatmeal.

Serve in small individual bowls. A spoon may be used or sip it from the bowl.

SURPRISE SOUP
Gu Tuk

SERVES 10

A traditional part of the Tibetan New Year is the making of gu tuk, two days before Losar morning. At this time there are many special pujas going on in the monasteries. This soup is traditionally made outdoors in a huge cauldron over an open fire. The elders preside over the making of the soup, stirring into it their wisdom, energy, and prayers. A long wooden pestle is used to mix the grain and vegetable base for this soup.

The most intriguing aspect of this soup is its symbolism. It combines folklore with auspicious coincidence. The tuk, or dumplings, for this soup are made into small spheres, like those in pa tuk (see p. 58) made for the full moon day. In a very large pot, there could well be hundreds of these in the soup. Nine of these dumplings contain a surprise inside.

These surprises consist of some small, natural object hidden inside the dough. The elder who is presiding over the gu tuk has written a list of these nine surprises and has attributed a quality to each. Each person who partakes of the soup has a chance to find a surprise in his or her bowl. How he or she relates to this discovery is up to them.

Some examples are incense for kindness, a coin for prosperity or generosity, charcoal for a black heart, mustard seed for a small mind. Other objects might be used: paper, wood, a gem stone, dried chili, a bit of cloth, a dried bean. A soup such as this is quite provocative, hopefully directing one toward introspection before the New Year.

The following is a recipe for a vegetarian version of gu tuk. You may let the elder in your household compose their list for the occasion. You will need a large stock pot for this soup.

INGREDIENTS:

4 cups unbleached white flour
water
1 cup barley
2 onion
2 cloves garlic
2 tablespoons ginger
2 vegetable bouillon cubes
4 plum tomatoes
6 stalks celery
6 carrots
4 large potatoes
8 mushrooms
1 bunch cilantro
olive oil

Make the dough by stirring cold water into the flour by hand until it becomes soft and workable. Set it aside, covered.

Wash, peel and chop all vegetables for the soup. Finely chop the ginger.

Sauté the onion, ginger, tomatoes, and mushrooms for 5 minutes.

Add the rest of the vegetables and the bouillon cubes. Add the barley and 12 cups of cold water, cooking over medium to high heat. While the soup is cooking prepare the noodles.

Roll the dough into a thick 'snake' about 1 inch in diameter. Pull off pieces with floured hands and roll them into balls. Many hands make for quick work.

Count the number of people in the family that are present for the soup. You may also include any absent family members who wish they were with you. For each person, make one round dumpling that is double the size of the others that are going into the soup. Set these aside to be filled with the tiny surprises.

When the soup is boiling and the vegetables are tender, add all the round dumplings, both the plain ones and those that are filled, and cook for another 15 to 20 minutes.

The elder of the household does the honors, ladling the soup into bowls, choosing one large dumpling for each bowl. When everyone is served and the prayers said, the eating fun begins. It is amazing how appropriate dumpling soup predictions can be!